Information Organization
& Dissemination
Through Subject Gateways

Information Organization & Dissemination Through Subject Gateways

By
DR. SUROJIT SANYAL

Ess Ess Publications
New Delhi

Information Organization & Dissemination Through Subject Gateways

Copyright © by Author

All rights reserved. No part of this book may be reproduced in any form or by any electronic or mechanical means including information storage and retrieval systems without permission in writing from the publisher, except by a reviewer, who may quote brief passages in a review.

While extensive effort has gone into ensuring the reliability of information appearing in this book, the publisher makes no warranty, express or implied on the accuracy or reliability of the information, and does not assume and hereby disclaims any liability to any person for any loss or damage caused by errors or omissions in this publication.

ISBN: 978-93-87698-86-4
Price : Rs. 600/-

First Published 2021

Published by:
Ess Ess Publications
4831/24, Ansari Road,
Darya Ganj,
New Delhi-110 002.
INDIA
Phones: 23260807, 41563444
Fax: 41563334
E-mail: info@essessreference.com
www.essessreference.com

Cover Design by *Patch Creative Unit*

Printed and bound in India

Declaration by Author

"Trademarked names may appear in this book. Rather than use a trademark symbol with every occurrence of a trademarked name, I use the names only in an editorial fashion and to the benefit of the trademark owner, with no intention of infringement of the trademark."

Contents

1	Introduction	1
2	Historical Background of the Subject Gateway	4
3	What is Subject Gateway	8
4	Review of Published Literature on Subject Gateways	12
5	Characteristics of Subject Gateways	40
6	Development of Subject Gateways Across the Ages	42
7	Problems Faced by Subject Gateways	127
8	How to Develop a Subject Gateway : A Step-by-Step Approach	131
Bibliography		137

1
Introduction

Along with the development of early writing method like "cuneiform" and other subsequent process of writing, people across the world had been trying to invent some cheap writing materials unlike clay, cloth, papyrus or parchment on which writing can be done easily. Paper was invented around 100 BC in China but industrial manufacturing of paper started in China in 105 AD. Paper turned out to be most affordable and easy writing material for the people around the world.

In 1440, Johannes Gutenberg of Germany invented printing press which revolutionised the process of printing. In 1455, "Gutenberg Bible" was first book that was printed through this printing press. Gutenberg was also pioneered for introduction of oil based ink for this movable type printing press.

Thereafter, rapid production of cost effective books started all over the world and libraries across the world started to collect these books for dissemination of information resulting expansion of libraries across the world. Then people across the society had the access to the library and its books resulted paradigm shift in information sharing.

But, libraries across the world had been witnessing new problems for organising these huge numbers of books. They were quite aware that unless they systematically organise the books and other documents, they would not be able to distribute them to the information seekers. In order to facilitate the same, different classification schemes started to evolve around the world. Then libraries started to adopt different classification schemes for classification of books and other printed materials as per their requirements.

In early 19th Century, Charles Babbage originated the concept of programmable computing device and invented the first mechanical computer. Meanwhile, Alexander Graham Bell invented telephone in 1876. Next 200 years witnessed gradual development of computers and communication technology in terms of speed, functionality and storage capacity. If we consider that the discovery of fire as first revolution, discovery of wheel as second revolution, then invention of computer and telephone may be considered as third revolution to the mankind. Practically every areas of our society is revolutionised with the application of computers and communication technology popularly known as IT and ICT.

Library as a social institution is also overwhelmed with the rapid developments of IT and ICT as large numbers of documents (both print and digital) have been generated through out the world along with these technological developments. Organization and dissemination of such huge number of documents (both print and digital) became a problem for most of the libraries, as conventional methods of organization and dissemination proved to be inadequate. As a result, conventional libraries started to change their conventional methods of organising, searching and disseminating of the information. They changed their conventional card catalogue to Online Public Access Catalogue (OPAC), manual circulation system to Integrated Library Management System (ILMS), Manual Indexing to Automated Indexing methods, and Conventional storage to Institutional Repository etc. But rapid growth digital

Introduction

documents resulted information overload. Therefore conventional search engine failed to provide desired search results as it contains more recall and less precision output.

Beginning of the Information Age was stared from August 1991, as the first web browser was released on the internet for general public. Along with the advancement of information age, information needs of the information seekers have also changed. Now more and more people wanted to have their desired information (preferably customised) available on their personal devices such as desktop, laptop, smart-phone etc. Hence we have to develop such a single-window information dissemination tool which will provide customised updated information on 24×7 basis to every information seeker. This information will be written by subject experts and organised by information experts for effective dissemination. Development of subject information gateways on different subjects might be a probable solution to the above mentioned challenges.

2
Historical Background of the Subject Gateway

As the computers became cheaper and its usage became more cost-effective, computerized database started evolving since 1960. In 1963[1], Charles William Bachman III, an American computer scientist, developed an early database management systems named Integrated Data Store (IDS), popularly known as navigational database model. There were two early navigational database model (i.e. the hierarchical model and the network database model). In 1970 [2], Edgar F. Codd, an English computer scientist, invented the relational model for database management. Thereafter the growth of the records was exponential in those databases. Along with the growth of the records, expansion of databases in terms of numbers, types and diversity (different subjects) was also observed in coming decades.

"The number of databases available to the public has grown by a factor of ten in the past 10 years".[3]   — **(Williams, 1986)**

But the searching technique differs from database to database. Ordinary users of these databases had been facing increased complexities in search techniques because of variety and variability of such databases. Researcher in the field of information science had been trying to develop a system which will provide easy access to information by providing simple searching technique to retrieve information from any database. Over the past few years, several new technologies appeared for the delivery of databases and to simplify its access and usage.

"Many studies have shown most people never learn how to use libraries or other information sources effectively" [4]

— (Tiefel, 1991)

But the proliferation of information and its importance has increased along with the passage of time. With the advancement of Information Technology (IT), it has become necessary for every individual to learn information searching mechanism and become an independent user of information. Information literacy is one such skill that could save an ordinary information seeker from being overburdened with the problems evolved due to information explosion. Libraries especially librarians are one of the major facilitators for imparting information literacy skills to the library users.

In 1990, a knowledge-based "Gateway" project was designed and developed for the students of Ohio State University's (OSU). In order to provide easy access to information, significant changes were made in this gateway after detailed evaluations of this project. Gateway users found it very easy to operate without any kind of orientation [5]. **(Tiefel, 1991)**

Meanwhile, English scientist Tim Berners-Lee invented the World Wide Web in 1989. He wrote the first web browser computer program in 1990. It marks the beginning of Information Age. Information has been proliferated leaps and bounds all over the world leading to Information explosion **(World Wide Web Foundation, 2018)**[6]. Along with the development of World Wide Web; search engines and web directories have also started emerging to control the downpour of information. Their main functions were Web Crawling,

Indexing and Searching. In 1993, web's first primitive search engine, "W3 Catalog" was released **(Nierstrasz, 1996)**[7]. Rapid developments of ICT helped the exponential growth of information both in physical and digital format. Moreover, paradigm shift of user's information needs calls for customized information service. But search engines and web directories fail to deliver desired results as these search results are of high recall value but of low precision **(Place, 2000)**[8]. Since mid-1990s, the volume of information resources on internet continued to grow exponentially. As a result the search engines and internet directories were unable to provide desired search result due to information overload **(Morville & Wickhorst, 1996)**[9]. Morville and Wickhorst provided step-by-step method for building subject-specific guide to help users in searching information resources on the Internet. An investigation conducted on library and related provision in UK's higher education institutions. Based on which 'Follett Report' was published in 1993. As per the recommendation of the report, Electronic Libraries Programme (eLib) was started in 1994. It was a £15m UK government initiative for utilizing Information Technology (IT) in the storage and retrieval process of information for betterment of Higher Education **(Higher Education Funding Councils, 1993)**[10]. Simultaneously, number of subject gateways on different subjects (i.e. chemistry, engineering, medicine etc.) started evolving across USA and UK after 1995. **(Krishnamurthy, 2005 July)**[11] Internet Public Library, a multi subject gateway, was established on 17th March, 1995 by School of Information of University of Michigan, USA. In India, development of subject gateways started late compared to UK, USA and other developed countries. In 1998, 'SciGate' was the first subject gateway established by Indian Institute of Science (IISc), Bangalore.

REFERENCE

1. Wikipedia. (2020). *Charles Bachman*. Retrieved from *https://en.wikipedia.org/wiki/Charles_Bachman* on 09/04/2020

2. Wikipedia. (2020). *Database*. Retrieved from *https://en.wikipedia.org/wiki/Database* on 10/04/2020

3. Williams, M. E. (1986). Transparent information systems through gateways, front ends, intermediaries and interfaces. *Journal of the American Society for Information Science, 37*(4), 204-214.

4. Tiefel, V. (1991). The gateway to information: A system redefines how libraries are used. *American Libraries, 22*(9), 858-860. Retrieved from *http://www.jstor.org/stable/25632371* accessed on 26.01.2017

5. Tiefel, V. (1991). The gateway to information: A system redefines how libraries are used. *American Libraries, 22*(9), 858-860. Retrieved from *http://www.jstor.org/stable/25632371* accessed on 26.01.2017

6. World Wide Web Foundation. (2018). *History of the web*. Retrieved from *http://webfoundation.org/about/vision/history-of-the-web/* accessed on 19.04.2020

7. Nierstrasz, O. (1996). *W3 catalog history*. Retrieved from *http://scg.unibe.ch/archive/software/w3catalog/W3CatalogHistory.html* accessed on 19.04.2020

8. Place, E. (2000). International collaboration on internet subject gateways. *IFLA Journal, 26*(1), 52-56. doi: 10.1177/034003520002600108

9. Morville, P. S., & Wickhorst, S. J. (1996). Building subject-specific guides to internet resources. *Internet Research, 6*(4), 27-32. doi: 10.1108/10662249610152276

10. Higher Education Funding Council for England. (1993). *Joint Funding Council's Libraries Review Group: Report (The Follett Report)*. Retrieved from *http://www.ukoln.ac.uk/services/papers/follett/report/* accessed on 19.04.2020

11. Krishnamurthy, M. (2005, July). Designing a gateway interface: Conceptual framework for library and information science. *Information Studies, 11*(3), 195-204.

3
What is Subject Gateway

In order to increase the effectiveness of libraries in UK, a review was conducted in 1992 by Higher Education Funding Council for England. Various recommendations were given in this review report, popularly known as 'The Follett Report'. As per their recommendations, different initiatives were taken across UK and USA. Among those initiatives, development of subject gateway for study and research is one of them. After 1995, subject gateways on different subjects started to come up around the world. (**Higher Education Funding Council for England, 1993**)[1]

In 1999, Robinson and Bawden in their review mentioned that

There is no precise definition of a subject gateway........ Unlike search engines, whose indexes are automatically constructed by software agents following automated identification of resources, gateway resources are selected intellectually by human experts. Explicit, and often strict, criteria are applied in the selection of resources, and the resources thus chosen are described and classified and/or indexed by the same human experts. Resources are selected on two general counts: appropriateness of subject content, and quality of the information resource. (**Robinson & Bawden, 1999**)[2]

In 2002, Bawden and Robinson again reviewed and defined subject gateway as:

> "Internet subject gateways are a tool for Internet resource discovery. They are best regarded as an example of a tertiary information source: guides to information resources, pointing to primary and secondary sources, and themselves pointed to by quaternary sources".
> — (Bawden & Robinson, 2002; p.157)[3]

Different experts and different subject gateway projects defined subject gateway in different point of time. Some of them are as follows:

Koch (2000)[4] defined the subject gateways as follows:

Subject gateways are Internet services which support systematic resource discovery. They provide links to resources (documents, objects, sites or services), predominantly accessible via the Internet. The service is based on resource description. Browsing access to the resources via a subject structure is an important feature. (p. 24-25)

Place (2000)[5] explained the subject gateways as follows:

Subject gateways are Internet-based services designed to help users locate high quality information that is available on the Internet. They are typically, databases of detailed metadata (or catalogue) records which describe Internet resources and offer a hyperlink to the resources. Users can choose to either search the database by keyword, or to browse the resources under subject headings. (p.53)

Kanetkar (2014)[6] described the definition of subject gateways given by **IMesh Toolkit Project** as follows:

A subject gateway is a website that provides searchable and browsable access to online resources focused around a specific subject. Subject gateway resource descriptions are usually created manually rather than being generated via an automated process. As the resource entries are generated by hand, they are usually superior to those available from a conventional web search engine. (p.367)

Definition of subject gateways given by **DESIRE Project** as follows:

"Selective subject gateways on the internet are characterized by their quality control. The core activities of resource selection and description rely on skilled human input (by librarians, academics and experts) and are not activities that lend themselves to automation." **(Kanetkar, 2014, p.367)**[7]

From the above definitions we may summarize the definition **(Sanyal, 2019)**[8] as follows:

"Subject Gateways are information sharing tools disseminate high quality information available over internet through their websites or portals. Gateways are developed with the joint effort of subject experts and information professionals for providing updated and qualitative online contents (sometime hyperlinked) focused on a specialised subject. Contents of the gateways can be searched through keywords or through relevant subject headings. Usually resource descriptions of the subject gateways are created manually rather than automated process, for providing better search results" (p.94)

REFERENCES

1. Higher Education Funding Council for England. (1993). *Joint Funding Council's Libraries Review Group: Report (The Follett Report).* Retrieved from *http://www.ukoln.ac.uk/services/papers/follett/report/* accessed on 19.04.2020
2. Robinson, L., & Bawden, D. (1999). Internet subject gateways. *International Journal of Information Management, 19*(6), 511-522.

3. Bawden, D., & Robinson, L. (2002). Internet subject gateways revisited. *International Journal of Information Management, 22,* 157–162.

4. Koch, T. (2000). Quality-controlled subject gateways: definitions, typologies, empirical overview. *Online Information Review, 24*(1), 24-34. doi: 10.1108/14684520010320040

5. Place, E. (2000). International collaboration on internet subject gateways. *IFLA Journal, 26*(1), 52-56. doi: 10.1177/034003520002600108

6. Kanetkar, J. (2014). Development of subject gateways: A status update. *DESIDOC Journal of Library & Information Technology, 34*(5), 367-375. doi: 10.14429/djlit.34.5807

7. Kanetkar, J. (2014). Development of subject gateways: A status update. *DESIDOC Journal of Library & Information Technology, 34*(5), 367-375. doi: 10.14429/djlit.34.5807

8. Sanyal, S. (2019). *Design and development of 'Jute-Gate': A prototype model of subject gateway on Jute information* (Doctoral dissertation, University of Calcutta).

4
Review of Published Literature on Subject Gateways

4.1. DEVELOPMENT OF SUBJECT GATEWAYS

4.1.1. Development of Subject Gateways across the World

The first database directory was published in 1976 **(Williams, Rouse, & Sandra, 1976)**[1]. The growth of records in those databases was exponential. Along with the growth of records in databases, growth in terms of variety and subject matter of databases was remarkable. Searching techniques of those databases differs with the variety of the databases. Over the past few years, several new technologies appeared for the delivery of databases and to simplify the access and use of online systems.

Williams provided an overview of the transparent information retrieval system and its needs. It was expressed that development of a total transparent information system for world knowledge is rarely possible. But subject gateways could provide a partial solution for such challenges **(Williams, 1986)**[2].

In 1990, a knowledge-based "Gateway" project was designed and developed for the students of Ohio State University's (OSU). In order to provide easy access to information, significant changes were made in this gateway after detailed evaluations of this project. Gateway users found it very easy to operate without any kind of orientation **(Tiefel, 1991)**[3].

Since mid-1990s, the volume of information resources on internet continued to grow exponentially. As a result the search engines and internet directories were unable to provide desired search result due to information overload **(Morville & Wickhorst, 1996)**[4]. Morville and Wickhorst provided step-by-step method for building subject-specific guide to help users in searching information resources on the Internet.

An investigation was conducted on library and related provision in UK's higher education institutions. Based on which 'Follett Report' was published in 1993. As per the recommendation of the report, Electronic Libraries Programme (eLib) was started in 1994. Under this program Art, Design, Architecture and Media (ADAM) gateway project was funded in the Access to Network Resources (ANR) category. The project was aimed to provide quality assured information on Art, Design, Architecture and Media through an information gateway. Bradshaw outlined the background of the ADAM project and also raised concerns about its future financial sustenance **(Bradshaw, 1997)**[5].

The mission of creating and operating continental-scale information services brought a whole new set of challenges. In 1998, Dixon, Melve, Meneses and Verschuren overviewed developing technologies which could be applied to address those challenges. They also investigated the extent to which these technologies had been successfully deployed in the Development of a European Service for Information on Research and Education (DESIRE) project **(Dixon, Melve, Meneses, & Verschuren, 1998)**[6].

Macleod, Kerr and Guyon outlined the need for a gateway to engineering information on the Internet. They also highlighted the background of the Edinburgh Engineering Virtual Library (EEVL) project. They compared certain similarities and differences in the development of EEVL and various other Subject Based Information Gateways (SBIGs) (i.e. ADAM, Social Science Information Gateway (SOSIG), and Organising Medical Networked Information (OMNI) gateway and similar services such as BUBL) **(Macleod, Kerr, & Guyon, 1998)**[7].

Priestley described "Vantage Points: Information gateways for business in the Yorkshire and Humber Region". Initially it was set up in 1997 at the University of Sheffield as part of the Telerise project. It was a simple database with links to the websites. Due to the changes in information retrieval techniques, these gateways were re-launched after incorporation of sophisticated services like harvesting and push technology **(Priestley, 1998)**[8].

One of the greatest challenges for users was to learn how the Internet could be used to meet their information needs and to conceptualize how the different Internet search and retrieval tools could help them to do this. Worsfold aimed to describe how subject gateways could help different user communities to make effective use of the Internet and to clarify some of the key differences between subject gateways and search engines **(Worsfold, 1998)**[9].

Griffith University and Queensland University of Technology Libraries, Australia jointly developed the project InfoQuest. This subject gateway was designed to help information seekers with appropriate information resources in their subject area. This searchable gateway contains brief records describing high quality information resources. All resources included in InfoQuest were evaluated by subject specialist for its content, scope, authority, ease-of-use and reliability of access **(Fredline & Reis, 1999)**[10].

SOSIG was a subject gateway to social science information on the Internet. SOSIG aimed to provide users with quick access to high-quality and useful information by selecting only valuable and scholarly Internet resources and making them available to users as an online catalogue. The selection saves users the effort and time of searching a possibly vast amount of irrelevant material. If first-time users found the gateways useful, then they would use them continuously and possibly they would check the gateways first before other means. In this report, Kuk examined how issues relating to quality and coverage would affect first-time users of SOSIG in deciding whether they would use it as a resource for their research **(Kuk, 1999)**[11].

Internet subject gateways were set up under the eLib programme to address information searching problems on the Internet. Mackie and Burton examined the usage pattern of academics in two universities used three eLib subject gateways (EEVL, OMNI and SOSIG). The results were encouraging for the eLib programme, but it was necessary for the gateways to be more effectively promoted. It was found that a large number of academics use the Internet frequently as part of teaching and research activities. Many academics feel that they require more orientation of the Internet along with other more familiar information-finding tools **(Mackie & Burton, 1999)**[12].

In this paper authors reviewed and described the development of subject gateways as discovery tools for internet resources. According to them, subject gateways are value added products which require intellectual efforts. They discussed the history and current status of subject gateways in UK. They also elaborated the nature and characteristics of subject gateways. According to them most subject gateways were developed by a small group of subject specialists and information professionals of an institution with subject relevance. Although collaboration was an increasing trend, still a few gateways were maintained by enthusiastic individuals **(Robinson & Bawden, 1999)**[13].

During 1998-99, several subject gateway projects were funded by the Australian Research Council. The key issues discussed in this paper were content creation, integration of access to print and electronic resources, archiving and persistent identification, sustainability and service integration. Though the subject gateways in Australia were relatively new compared to the European experience, still their efforts regarding provision of high quality Web resources had been very useful. According to Campbell, International consensus in the development of subject gateway was needed to avoid redundancy in research discipline **(Campbell, 2000)**[14].

Gateways had been developing a range of services to become a mature one. A range of parallel and alternative services had been emerging. Gateways had been introducing those alternate services in order to financially sustain themselves. Gateways were trying to reduce funding burden by way of partnership and commercial engagement. In this paper, Dempsey discussed the critical importance of discovery and disclosure services and also suggested how gateways might position themselves in the shared network environment **(Dempsey, 2000)**[15].

Heery discussed the possible implications of cooperation on different areas of subject based gateways. The areas of cooperation included coverage policy, creation of metadata, and provision of searching and browsing across services **(Heery, 2000)**[16].

Cooperative Online Resource Catalogue (CORC) being an Online Computer Library Centre (OCLC) project developed a system for hosting and supporting subject gateways than a gateway itself. It mainly relied on large-scale cooperation among libraries to maintain a centralized database. CORC widened scope of libraries and librarians by supporting metadata standards like Dublin Core, Unicode and Resource Description Framework (RDF) **(Hickey, 2000)**[17].

Koch described subject gateways where a set of quality measures were taken for systematic resource discovery. In quality-controlled subject gateways, considerable amount of human efforts were given for selection of quality resources. In order to ensuring good collection, regular checking and update was needed. For effective searching and browsing of quality resources on a particular subject, controlled vocabularies and deep classification structure were prepared **(Koch, 2000)**[18].

Peereboom overviewed the design and organisation of Dutch Electronic Subject Service (DutchESS). It was created as a national collaborative effort among National Library and other academic libraries. The model of DutchESS was discussed with reference to its selection policy, metadata format, classification scheme and retrieval options **(Peereboom, 2000)**[19].

Subject gateways such as Social Science Information Gateway (SOSIG) had been available on the Internet for some years and they offer an alternative to Internet search engines and directories. Place suggested that librarians would be the ideal person to play a major role in building Internet resource discovery services. She outlined some of the subject gateway initiatives in Europe and also described the tools and technologies developed by the Development of a European Service for Information on Research and Education (DESIRE) project to support the development of new gateways in other countries **(Place, 2000)**[20].

Veterinary and agricultural libraries of the five Nordic countries - Denmark, Finland, Iceland, Norway and Sweden produced NOVAGate in 1998. This gateway covers Nordic and European resources as well as the resources of international organizations on agricultural, veterinary and related fields **(Price, 2000)**[21].

In order to access information in electronic environments, subject gateways must support all three stages in the organisation of knowledge (i.e. selection, organisation, and de-selection). The three principles in relation to organization of knowledge that emerge are (a) Knowledge organization for communities, (b) Tools for knowledge organization must be designed in accordance with user orientation and predominant usage (c) Standardisation and networking infrastructures facilitates for efficient access to information. According to Rowley, Processes and tools for organization of knowledge need to be perfect according to the needs of the community **(Rowley, 2000)**[22].

Renardus was a collaborative project of the EU's Information Society programme with partners from national libraries, university research and technology centres and subject gateways across Europe. Its aim was to build a single window service allowing users to search and browse existing Internet-accessible scientific and cultural resource collections distributed across Europe. Renardus evolved a collaborative model for addressing the increasingly difficult issues of sustainability and scalability facing individual gateway services. Huxley outlined the opportunities and benefits for future collaboration with other organizations in developing the fully operational service **(Huxley, 2001)**[23].

Subject based information gateways (SBIG) are organized collections of networked information. They provide a searchable and brows-able catalogue of authoritative Internet resources to the users. Monopoli and Nicholas provided an evaluation of the Art, Design, Architecture and Media Gateway (ADAM) gateway. It provided information about its users, its services, search methods etc. **(Monopoli & Nicholas, 2001)**[24].

Neuroth and Koch presented a mapping process to define a common metadata format for cross-searching distributed and heterogeneous subject gateways. EU project-Renardus had a well-defined data model with semantic and syntactical definitions of each metadata element. It resulted in richer and semantically controlled cross-searching. The metadata elements were based on Dublin Core. In order to create a well-structured description of each participating gateway, a collection level description schema was also been developed. The experience gathered from Renardus and some of its solutions might be used at similar interoperability efforts **(Neuroth & Koch, 2001)**[25].

Powell considered the use of the Open Archives Initiative Protocol for Metadata Harvesting as a mechanism for sharing metadata records between these gateways. This would help in creation of cross-subject resource discovery services **(Powell, 2001)**[26].

Bawden and Robinson reviewed and believed that the subject gateways had been an under-valued and under-utilized. Important task for information specialists was to promote the value of these subject gateways. International developments along with increasing importance of gateways in higher education would help in overcoming this problem **(Bawden & Robinson, 2002)**[27].

Interoperability was an indispensable issue among knowledge organization systems. Various methods were used in achieving the same. Mapping was one such intellectual method. Both human mapping and computer-aided mapping would coexist in near future. It was beyond doubt that the need for integrating different subject vocabularies in the networked environment is essential **(Chan & Zeng, 2002)**[28].

Information needs are dynamic. The Australasian Virtual Engineering Library (AVEL) had taken iterative approach to interface design, usability testing and customer needs analysis. User-centred design had ensured AVEL remains relevant to its target audience. In this paper Clark and Frost described the methodologies employed by (AVEL) to discover the needs of customers. Repeated evaluation and scenario based testing was found to be useful analysis tools. Conclusions for future development were drawn based on the results of usability study and responses to customer demands (Clark & Frost, 2002)[29].

Unlike Internet directories, resource descriptions in Subject Gateways were of high quality. It would be useful to researchers, academics and other professionals in the specific subject field and also to the wider community. However, Freshwater suggested that sustainability is one future problem that Gateways would face **(Freshwater, 2002)**[30].

There was growing demand for a wide range of search aids considering the scale and variety of information provided. When keyword indexing was the only option then spelling variation, updated terminology, foreign language phrases and contextually ambiguous terms could lead to false positive retrieval. A thesaurus of subject terms could enhances searching precision by eliminating false leads. Heron and Hanson discussed about the efficient retrieval technique with the use of uniform metadata format by using thesauri and authority files **(Heron & Hanson, 2003)**[31].

Quality-controlled subject gateways support systematic resource discovery. Thirion, Loosli, Douyère and Darmon proposed several metadata element sets to describe, index and qualify health resources to be included in a French quality controlled health gateway called French acronym for Catalogue and Index of French Language Health Resources (CISMeF). The Dublin Core metadata element set was used in CISMeF to enhance Internet health document retrieval and navigation, and to allow interoperability **(Thirion, Loosli, Douyère, & Darmoni, 2003)**[32].

UK based subject gateway SOSIG was facing two key challenges (a) the sustainability of a labour intensive service and (b) innovation and evaluation needed to keep pace with user needs. Huxley and Joyce analysed and found that in order to face the challenges SOSIG needed to take a more strategic approach for future sustainability through collaboration, service design and user engagement **(Huxley & Joyce, 2004)**[33].

Increasing number of information resources stressed the need for meta-search capabilities which enable users to simultaneous search of heterogeneous information resources. Sadeh addressed three issues (a) Availability of metadata to meta-search system, (b) Convertibility of unified query by meta-search system and (c) Creation of Local indexes for accessing some repositories which were not available to the meta-search system **(Seadh, 2004)**[34].

Day, Koch and Neuroth described Renardus cross-search and cross-browse service which was based on the Z39.50 protocol. They reviewed the data models for coming up with a common model consisting of minimum set of Dublin Core-based metadata elements for the Renardus service. This model provided the basic infrastructure for interoperability between the participating gateways. They also described how the mapping of information was used to aid end-user navigation in deep subject-browsing structures. Renardus developed interesting ways of browsing large subject structures with the help of classification hierarchies **(Day, Koch, & Neuroth, 2005)**[35].

Kaczmarek and ChiatNaun investigated the feasibility of unified searching across multiple information sources through use of the Open Archives Initiative Protocol for Metadata Harvesting (OAI PMH) in tandem with the Z39.50 protocol. A meta-search service model was constructed based on the Z39.50/OAI Gateway Profile. But it was concluded that the Z39.50/OAI Gateway Profile could not be deployed for limitations of Z servers **(Kaczmarek & ChiatNaun, 2005)**[36].

Caswell described guided search technology in subject gateway to improve users' access to electronic resources by shortening the pathway to information. This was an innovative and useful search interfaces, especially for inexperienced users. Caswell only focused on the technical aspects involved in creating guided searches though it did not addressed the use of usability testing **(Caswell, 2006)**[37].

Gabriel, the worldwide web server of European national libraries, had been providing a single point gateway to information about their functions, services and collections. Three national libraries participated in the pilot project. The national libraries of the United Kingdom, Netherlands, Finland and Germany participated through an international project to develop the service. Gabriel turned out to be a model for collaboration **(Jefcoate, 2006)**[38].

Specialized subject gateways became an essential tool for locating and accessing digital information resources. A prototype model for developing software tool was developed that enables subject gateways to be developed and managed. Using Dublin Core proved to be the best option for the treatment of metadata **(Tramullas & Garrido, 2006)**[39].

Uddin, Mezbah-ul-Islam and Haque defined the recent developments in classification structure and its role in organizing and finding information. According to them appropriate use of classification structure would serve as an effective tool for information retrieval. They explained Information description and discovery in web with a case study. It was found that hierarchical-enumerative structure was most suitable for subject gateways. As a user oriented classification on the Web, folksonomy emerged as another viable approach **(Uddin, Mezbah-ul-Islam, & Haque, 2006)**[40].

The popularity of Subject Based Information Gateways (SBIGs) became very popular because of human intervention in the process of content creation and in the search process. The main aims of SBIGs were to supply quality controlled information resources within a limited time. In future, more efforts would be given on the specialization, efficiency and accuracy of e-Services to wider audiences. Collaborative efforts among SBIGs would be viable solution in the areas of exchange of records, cross searching, mirroring remote service, cooperative digital reference service, online tutorials etc. **(Huang & Liu, 2007)**[41].

Zygogiannis, Papatheodorou, Chandrinos and Makropoulos reported that conventional search engines were insufficient in context-sensitive query answering, subject gateways had been considered as the qualitative response to information overload **(Zygogiannis, Papatheodorou, Chandrinos, & Makropoulos, 2009)**[42].

Caswell and Wynstra reviewed the evolving nature of library web sites. They described the milestones in the development of a library gateway and the integration of federated search into the gateway **(Caswell & Wynstra, 2010)**[43].

Matthew and others showed that in subject indexing, tagging increase the effectiveness of non-specialist users in a knowledge organisation system **(Matthews, Jones, Puzoñ, Moon, Tudhope, Golub, & Lykke, 2010)**[44].

Anil Hirwade investigated and analysed the metadata standards available worldwide. It helped him in comparing and adopting required standard for the repositories. As existing metadata was unable to cover required facets, an implementer was required to create a new scheme with the desired metadata elements. But it would create issues in interoperating. Creating an extra element would fill the gaps in the coverage. The problem of interoperability could be solved by publications of new elements, declaring their definitions, formats, etc. **(Anil Hirwade, 2011)**[45].

Wang talked about the four key techniques of subject gateway service (i.e. information organization technology, meta-searching technique, XML technique and computer security technique). Wang concluded that people were less concern about utilization of subject information gateway because of their lack of knowledge **(Wang, 2011)**[46].

In December 2009, CIPRES Science Gateway (CSG) was released with the aims to provide browser-based access to phylogenetic code. The steady growth in resource use suggested that the CSG had been meeting the needs of the Systematic/ Evolutionary Biology community. Miller, Pfeiffer, and Schwartz concluded that CSG had been a critical and cost-effective enabler of science for phylogenetic researchers **(Miller, Pfeiffer, & Schwartz, 2012)**[47].

CONCLUSION

The review of literature pertaining to subject gateways was undertaken using both relevant journals (both print and online) and electronic databases in order to ascertain the historical and present status of subject gateways. **Bradshaw (1997)**[48] and **Dempsey (2000)**[49] raised concerns about financial sustenance which had been one of the prime issues since the beginning of Subject Gateway. Different methods, technologies, tools, services have been developed all over the world to enhance the quality and service of subject gateways. It was found that hierarchical-enumerative structure was most suitable for information retrieval in subject gateways **(Uddin, et al., 2006)**[50]. According to **Huang and Liu (2007)**[51] more efforts should be given on the specialization, efficiency and accuracy of e-Services to wider audiences in future. Hierarchical-enumerative structure of Jute taxonomy would be used for effective information and retrieval. Moreover a micro subject like Jute was chosen for deeper exploration and access to specialized knowledge domain.

4.1.2. Development of Subject Gateways in India

Singh and Gautam (2003)[52] suggested that developing subject gateways in specific areas is one of the effective and efficient ways of providing easy access to quality information on internet. Information requirement of the scientific and academic community could be satisfied through these subject specific gateways.

Krishnamurthy (2005 July)[53] felt that human intervention is needed to guide in the search process. According to him gateways could improve the effectiveness of internet searching. In order to provide more enhanced retrieval options for internet users, he stressed the need for the integration of metadata in particular Dublin Core. He felt that awareness about subject gateways among academics and researchers would help in greater usage. SciGate was developed in 2001 by the Indian Institute of Science (IISc), Bangalore. Scope of the SciGate contents and its navigation interface was revised based on the feedback from its user.

Mahemei, Thulasi and Rajashekar found that Taxonomies' has been a useful approach to address the different design aspects of information portals. They defined the scope of taxonomy based on the user needs and then outlined it. They also discussed about the implementation of the revised SciGate architecture **(Mahemei, Thulasi, & Rajashekar, 2005)**[54].

MasoomRaza and Eqbal described the LISgateway: India's the first gateway in the field of library and information science. In 2004, the project was sponsored by the University Grants Commission (UGC) of New Delhi, India. The prime aim of this project was to provide a trusted source of selected, high-quality Internet information in the field of library and information science and promote e-resources resulted from research and teaching **(MasoomRaza & Eqbal, 2005)**[55].

Lalhmachhuana described the emergence of Subject Information Gateways and highlighted their role and significance in the present era of proliferation of information on the Internet. He also suggested some methods for promoting the use of Subject Information Gateways **(Lalhmachhuana, 2006)**[56].

On deeper analysis of available technologies and strategies, Vijayakumar and Ganesan found that there had been considerable overlap between information gateways, portals and virtual libraries etc. User's dependency on different search engines had been prevalent due to lack of a collaborated gateway. They proposed a study for the development of a global subject gateway portal with the help of an internationally integrated search strategy and content management system **(Vijayakumar & Ganesan, 2006)**[57].

Madhusudhan conducted a study to assess trends of information search by research scholars and the problems faced by them while doing so. It was found that they used search engines more than that of web directories or subject gateways as they did not know about subject gateways or web directories **(Madhusudhan, 2007)**[58].

Gul in his dissertation, evaluated and organized different web resources on Social Science by designing a model subject gateway **(Gul, 2009)**[59].

Munshi addressed the issues of interoperability among digital repositories which were flooded with information due to the adoption of information and communication technology. With the help of these repositories, subject gateways could provide single window dissemination of scholarly information. Such initiatives would help in building information infrastructure for library and information network **(Munshi, 2009)**[60].

The availability of e-resources and conventional resources was increased in huge numbers on specific subject domain. As a result subject based content collection gateways had been flourishing all around the globe. Neelakandan, Malatesh and Surulinathi explained about a gateway on Biotechnology. They explained the need and scope of creating a subject based information gateway on specific subject content such as Biotechnology, Nanotechnology etc. **(Neelakandan, Malatesh, & Surulinathi, 2010)**[61].

Rajashekara discussed brief background of the subject gateways and the development of BT-Gate. He focused on different online electronic resources available in the field of biotechnology which had been covered in BT-Gate **(Rajashekara, 2010)**[62].

Kumar and Singh tried to assess usefulness of e-resources and also monitored the skills of the Scientists of National Physical Laboratory while using various search methods and techniques for accessing and utilizing these e-resources. They measured the level of satisfaction and various challenges faced by scientists while searching e-resources. The findings revealed that access and use of information was an important component of research activities. Simple search techniques and self-taught methods were mostly used to access the e-information from E-journals. Research also indicated that internet was most preferred medium of accessing e-information. Kumar and Singh suggested that Libraries should develop their own subject gateways, portals and data archives for moving towards a brighter future **(Kumar & Singh, 2011)**[63].

Pommi suggested for developing a gateway for world digital libraries where available knowledge bases would be filtered and placed into a system to have easy access to the information **(Pommi, 2011)**[64].

'Online Reference Zone', a gateway of open source online reference sources on science and technology, was designed, developed and hosted at the Indian Statistical Institute, Bangalore centre library. Meera and Ummer explained the process of developing online reference gateway in selected subjects like Physics, Chemistry, etc. They explained federated search facility and also an additional feature in which the user could submit relevant links related to the site **(Meera & Ummer, 2012)**[65].

Sureshkumar developed a single window interface on physics and allied subjects. Through this physics gateway he wanted to provide full-text scholarly information available on the web to the researcher in physics. He analysed the thrust areas of research on physics and also filtered resources for physics to promote research. He also stressed the need for updating of the Physics portal on regular basis to make it sustainable in future **(Sureshkumar, 2012)**[66].

Bhardwaj discussed about the importance, objective, scope and interdisciplinary relevance of gateway in academic libraries. He explained the steps involved in building a gateway. Besides this, OAI-PMH and Z39.50 standards, architecture and features of the knowledge gateway were also discussed **(Bhardwaj, 2013)**[67].

Subject gateway service came into existence along with the development of internet especially World Wide Web (WWW). Rapid proliferation of digital resources compelled the libraries across the world initiate subject specific customized information dissemination services for its users. Kanetkar reviewed the development of subject gateways from 1999 till 2013 and discussed the most critical features expected from a subject gateway **(Kanetkar, 2014)**[68].

Manivel compiled a web based information source on physical science for students, researches and researchers of Bharathidsaan University. It was necessary to systematically list physics information resources scattered in various websites. Therefore an attempt was made to identify various sources and to record the same through this study. It included books, journal articles and related websites **(Manivel, 2014)**[69].

Information overload put serious challenges before Libraries and information centres for effectively satisfying information needs of the users. Access to online sources would not serve its purpose until and unless the users were informed about its utilization. Limited budget, increased demand for information and limited time for disposal of information made huge scope for such portals as they have been providing customized information services through a single window. Thirupathi in his dissertation also suggested future plans to update the Mathematics & Statistics portal on a regular basis in order to satisfy demands of the users **(Thirupathi, 2014)**[70].

Subject based content collection gateways had been

increasing around the globe. Vijayaselvi and Natarajan explained one such gateway on Mathematical science. Vijayaselvi and Natarajan explained the need and scope of creating mathematical subject based gateway. They presented the goal, principle and contents for constructing web portal on Mathematics. The resource selection criteria and standards for web-based resource description were also been described **(Vijayaselvi & Natarajan, 2014)**[71].

Information seekers accessed concerned subject gateways for ensuring quality information. As anything produced in the knowledge industry without human intervention is dangerous, therefore librarians would have to play a very crucial role in this regard. They must ensure the availability of authentic sources in order to maintain the quality of such gateways. Subject gateway on chemistry was developed as a demonstration for the systematic resource discovery and dissemination for online information **(Yuvaraja, 2014)**[72].

CONCLUSION

The aim of this part of literature review is to measure the knowledge exploration already done on Subject Gateways in India. **Singh and Gautam (2003)**[73] suggested that an effective and efficient way to provide easy access to quality information on internet is by developing subject gateways in specific areas. Therefore, development of a model prototype subject gateway on jute fibre is proposed. Mahemei and others found that 'Taxonomies' offer a useful approach to address the different design aspects of information portals **(Mahemei et al., 2005)**[74]. Vijayakumar and Ganesan proposed a study on the development of a subject gateway with a content management system **(Vijayakumar & Ganesan, 2006)**[75]. It was found that information seekers used search engines more than that of web directories or subject gateways as they did not know about subject gateways **(Madhusudhan, 2007)**[76]. Munshi addressed the issues of interoperability among digital repositories which will help subject gateways to provide dissemination of single window scholarly information **(Munshi, 2009)**[77]. In actual development, when Jute-Gate will be developed with participating institutions on consortia model, interoperability of the repositories among the participating institutions is needed for easy accessing of relevant information. **Kumar and Singh (2011)**[78] tried to measure the usefulness of e-resources and suggested that Libraries should develop their own subject gateways and **Bhardwaj (2013)**[79] explained the steps involved in building the subject gateway. **Kanetkar (2014)**[80] reviewed the development of subject gateways from 1999 till 2013 and discussed the most critical features expected from a subject gateway. On the basis of this review, a further literature review of subject gateways from 1996 to 2017 was conducted to measure the actual status of the gateways across the world.

4.2. REVIEW OF SUBJECT GATEWAYS

According to Koch, John Kirriemuir conducted a brief survey outside UK on "quality resource discovery systems" in 1999. The survey provided a list of 50 quality controlled gateways along with a couple of additions. It was found that most of the gateways were maintained and mounted on university based web servers. In most cases gateways were hosted and funded by academia. He raised the question of sustainability of the subject gateways **(Koch, 2000)**[87].

Robinson and Bawden reviewed, discussed and exemplified subject gateways available as on August 1999. They described subject gateways as discovery tools for online resources available over internet. In this paper, history and current status of subject gateways were discussed in detail. They also explained the nature and characteristics of subject gateways. According to them, subject gateways are value added product which requires intellectual efforts of subject specialist and informational professionals. Survey revealed that most subject gateways were developed by subject specialists and information professionals of the funding institution with the subject relevance. According to them, subject gateways developed through collaboration was an increasing trend, although, few gateways were maintained by individuals. They also provided a representative list of subject gateways existed as on August 1999 **(Robinson & Bawden, 1999)**[88].

Three years later, Bawden and Robinson further reviewed subject gateways **(Bawden & Robinson, 2002)**[89]. They review result made them belief that most of the subject gateways had been under-valued and under-utilized. It was the greater role of the information specialists to promote of the value of these subject gateways among information seekers. It would enhance the marketability of the gateway services among users. It would also help the subject gateway to sustain longer period. According to them, increasing importance of gateways in higher education, especially in research would help the subject gateways in overcoming this problem. Rapid growth of digital resources prompted libraries across the world for initiating tailor-made subject specific information dissemination services for its users.

Kanetkar (2014)[90] reviewed the development of 77 subject gateways across the world. The reference period of the survey was between 1999 till 2013. She also discussed the most critical features expected from a subject gateway.

REFERENCES

1. Williams, M. E., & Rouse, S. K. (Eds.). (1976). *Computer-readable bibliographic databases: A directory and data sourcebook.* Washington, D.C.: American Society for Information Science.
2. Williams, M. E. (1986). Transparent information systems through gateways, front ends, intermediaries and interfaces. *Journal of the American Society for Information Science, 37*(4), 204-214.
3. Tiefel, V. (1991). The gateway to information: A system redefines how libraries are used. *American Libraries, 22*(9), 858-860. Retrieved from

http://www.jstor.org/stable/25632371 accessed on 26.01.2017

4. Morville, P. S., & Wickhorst, S. J. (1996). Building subject-specific guides to internet resources. *Internet Research, 6*(4), 27-32. doi: 10.1108/10662249610152276

5. Bradshaw, R. (1997).Introducing ADAM: A gateway to internet resources in art, design, architecture and media. *Program, 31*(3), 251-267. doi:10.1108/eum0000000006889

6. Dixon, T., Melve, I., Meneses, R., & Verschuren, T. (1998). Building large-scale information services: Tools and experiences from the DESIRE project. *Computer Networks and ISDN Systems, 30*(16), 1559-1569. doi: 10.1016/S0169-7552(98)00190-1

7. Macleod, R., Kerr, L., & Guyon, A. (1998). The EEVL approach to providing a subject based information gateway for engineers. *Program, 32*(3), 205-223. doi: 10.1108/eum0000000006901

8. Priestley, A. (1998). Vantage points: Information gateways for business in the Yorkshire and Humber Region. *New Review of Information Networking, 4*(1), 213-216. doi:10.1080/13614579809516930

9. Worsfold, E. (1998). Subject gateways: Fulfilling the DESIRE for knowledge. *Computer Networks and ISDN Systems, 30*(16-18), 1479-1489. doi: 10.1016/S0169-7552(98)00185-8

10. Fredline, S., & Reis, B. (1999). Infoquest: Collaborative development of a subject resource gateway. *New Review of Information Networking, 5*(1), 125-130. doi: 10.1080/13614579909516941

11. Kuk, G. (1999). Social science information gateway for psychology: A utility test of SOSIG. Social Science Computer Review, 17(4), 451-454. doi: 10.1177/089443939901700405

12. Mackie, M., & Burton, P. F. (1999). The use and effectiveness of the eLib subject gateways: A preliminary investigation. *Program, 33*(4), 327-337. doi: 10.1108/eum0000000006922

13. Robinson, L. & Bawden, D. (1999). Internet subject gateways. *International Journal of Information Management, 19*(6), 511-522.

14. Campbell, D. (2000). Australian subject gateways: political and strategic issues. *Online Information Review, 24*(1), 73-77. doi: 10.1108/14684520010320266

15. Dempsey, L. (2000). The subject gateway: experiences and issues based on the emergence of the resource discovery network. *Online Information Review, 24*(1), 8-23. doi: 10.1108/14684520010323029

16. Heery, R. (2000). Information gateways: Collaboration on content. *Online Information Review, 24*(1), 40-45. doi: 10.1108/14684520010320077

17. Hickey, T. B. (2000). CORC: A system for gateway creation. *Online Information Review, 24*(1), 49-56. doi: 10.1108/14684520010371549

18. Koch, T. (2000). Quality-controlled subject gateways: definitions, typologies, empirical overview. *Online Information Review, 24*(1), 24-34. doi: 10.1108/14684520010320040

19. Peereboom, M. (2000). DutchESS: Dutch electronic subject service – a Dutch national collaborative effort. *Online Information Review, 24*(1), 46-49. doi:10.1108/14684520010320095

20. Place, E. (2000). International collaboration on internet subject gateways. *IFLA Journal, 26*(1), 52-56. doi: 10.1177/034003520002600108

21. Price, A. (2000). NOVAGate: A nordic gateway to electronic resources in the forestry, veterinary and agricultural sciences. *Online Information Review, 24*(1), 69-73. doi: 10.1108/14684520010320158

22. Rowley, J. (2000). Knowledge organisation for a new millennium: Principles and processes. *Journal of Knowledge Management, 4*(3), 217-223. doi: 10.1108/13673270010350011

23. Huxley, L. (2001). Renardus: Fostering collaboration between academic subject gateways in Europe. *Online Information Review, 25*(2), 121-127. doi: 10.1108/14684520110390060.

24. Monopoli, M., & Nicholas, D. (2001). A user evaluation of subject based information gateways: Case study ADAM. In *Aslib Proceedings* (Vol. 53, No.1, pp.39-52). MCB UP Ltd. doi: 10.1108/eum0000000007036

25. Neuroth, H., & Koch, T. (2001, October). Metadata mapping and application profiles: approaches to providing the cross-searching of heterogeneous resources in the EU project Renardus. In *International Conference on Dublin Core and Metadata Applications* (pp. 122-129). National Institute of Informatics, Tokyo, Japan. Retrieved from *http://dcpapers.dublincore.org/index.php/pubs/article/viewFile/650/646* accessed on 03.05.2020

26. Powell, A. (2001). An OAI approach to sharing subject gateway content. In *Tenth International World Wide Web Conference (WWW10)*. University of Bath. Retrieved from *https://researchportal.bath.ac.uk/files/617071/Powell.pdf* accessed on 03.05.2020

27. Bawden, D., & Robinson, L. (2002). Internet subject gateways revisited. *International Journal of Information Management, 22*(2), 157-162.

28. Chan, L. M., & Zeng, M. L. (2002). Ensuring interoperability among subject vocabularies and knowledge organization schemes: A

methodological analysis. *IFLA Journal, 28*(5-6), 323-327. Retrieved from *http://files.eric.ed.gov/fulltext/ED472886.pdf* accessed on 03.05.2020

29. Clark, N., & Frost, D. (2002). User-centred evaluation and design: A subject gateway perspective. In *11th VALA Conference, Melbourne* (pp. 6-8). Retrieved from *http://www.vala.org.au/vala2002/2002pdf/38ClaFro.pdf* accessed on 03.05.2020

30. Freshwater, M. (2002). Subject gateways: An investigation into their role in the information environment (with particular reference to AERADE, the subject gateway for aerospace and defence. (Master's dissertation, University of Central England)

31. Heron, S. J., & Hanson, A. (2003). From subject gateways to portals: The role of metadata in accessing international research. Retrieved from *http://scholarcommons.usf.edu/cgi/viewcontent.cgi?article=1011&context=dean_cbcs* accessed on 03.05.2020

32. Thirion, B., Loosli, G., Douyère, M., & Darmoni, S. J. (2003). Metadata element set in a quality-controlled subject gateway: A step to a health semantic web. Studies in Health Technology and Informatics, 707-712. Retrieved from *https://www.researchgate.net/profile/Gaelle_Loosli/publication/8969250_Metadata_element_set_in_a_Quality-Controlled_Subject_Gateway_a_step_to_an_health_semantic_Web/links/0deec533e7a26350c6000000.pdf* accessed on 03.05.2020

33. Huxley, L., & Joyce, A. (2004). A social science gateway in a shifting digital world: Shaping SOSIG for users' needs of the future. *Online Information Review, 28*(5), 328-337. doi: 10.1108/14684520410564253

34. Sadeh, T. (2004). The challenge of meta-searching. *New Library World, 105*(3/4), 104-112. doi: 10.1108/03074800410526721

35. Day, M., Koch, T., & Neuroth, H. (2005). Searching and browsing multiple subject gateways in the Renardus service. Retrieved from *http://opus.bath.ac.uk/14366/1/day-renardus-paper-v2.pdf* accessed on 03.05.2020

36. Kaczmarek, J., & ChiatNaun, C. (2005). A state-wide meta-search service using OAI-PMH and Z39.50. *Library Hi Tech, 23*(4), 576-586. doi: 10.1108/07378830510636355

37. Caswell, J. V. (2006). Leveraging resources in a library gateway. *Library Hi Tech, 24*(1), 142-152. doi: 10.1108/07378830510636391

38. Jefcoate, G. (2006). Gabriel: Gateway to Europe's national libraries. *Program, 40*(4), 325-333. doi: 10.1108/00330330610707908.

39. Tramullas, J., & Garrido, P. (2006). Constructing web subject gateways using dublin core, the resource description framework and

topic maps. *Information Research, 11*(2), 1-10. Retrieved from *http://eprints.rclis.org/7540/2/paper248.pdf* accessed on 04.05.2020

40. Uddin, M. N., Mezbah-ul-Islam, M., & Haque, K. M. G. (2006). Information description and discovery method using classification structures in web. *Malaysian Journal of Library and Information Science, 11*(2), 1-20. Retrieved from *https://mjlis.um.edu.my/article/view/7828/5383* accessed on 04.05.2020

41. Huang, R., & Liu, C. (2007). An investigation and analysis of e-services in major subject based information gateways in the world. In Integration and innovation orient to e-society Volume 2 (pp. 209-217). Springer Boston, MA. doi: 10.1007/978-0-387-75494-9_26

42. Zygogiannis, K., Papatheodorou, C., Chandrinos, K., & Makropoulos, K. (2009). Automatic web resource discovery for subject gateways. Retrieved from *https://www.researchgate.net/profile/Christos_Papatheodorou/publication/255582837_Automatic_Web_Resource_Discovery_for_Subject_Gateways/links/0f31753bfcd7fa7540000000.pdf* accessed on 04.05.2020

43. Caswell, J. V., & Wynstra, J. D. (2010). Improving the search experience: Federated search and the library gateway. *Library Hi Tech, 28*(3), 391-401. doi: 10.1108/07378831011076648

44. Matthews, B., Jones, C., Puzoñ, B., Moon, J., Tudhope, D., Golub, K., & Lykke Nielsen, M. (2010, July). An evaluation of enhancing social tagging with a knowledge organization system. In V. Broughton (Ed.), *Aslib Proceedings*, (Vol. 62, No. 4/5, pp. 447-465). Emerald Group Publishing Limited. doi: 10.1108/00012531011074690

45. Anil Hirwade, M. (2011). A study of metadata standards. *Library Hi Tech News, 28*(7), 18-25. doi: 10.1108/07419051111184052

46. Wang, L. (2011). A study of key techniques of subject information gateway service. In Advanced research on computer science and information engineering (pp. 183-187). Springer Berlin Heidelberg. doi: 10.1007/978-3-642-21411-0_30

47. Miller, M. A., Pfeiffer, W., & Schwartz, T. (2012). The CIPRES science gateway: enabling high-impact science for phylogenetics researchers with limited resources. In *Proceedings of the 1st conference of the extreme science and engineering discovery environment: Bridging from the extreme to the campus and beyond* (p. 39). ACM. doi: 10.1145/2335755.2335836

48. Bradshaw, R. (1997). Introducing ADAM: A gateway to internet resources in art, design, architecture and media. *Program, 31*(3), 251-267. doi: 10.1108/eum0000000006889

49. Dempsey, L. (2000). The subject gateway: experiences and issues based on the emergence of the resource discovery network. *Online*

Information Review, 24(1), 8-23. doi: 10.1108/14684520010323029

50. Uddin, M. N., Mezbah-ul-Islam, M., & Haque, K. M. G. (2006). Information description and discovery method using classification structures in web. *Malaysian Journal of Library and Information Science*, 11(2), 1-20. Retrieved from https://mjlis.um.edu.my/article/view/7828/5383 accessed on 04.05.2020

51. Huang, R., & Liu, C. (2007). An investigation and analysis of e-services in major subject based information gateways in the world. In *Integration and innovation orient to e-society volume 2* (pp. 209-217). Springer US. doi: 10.1007/978-0-387-75494-9_26

52. Singh, A., & Gautam, J. N. (2003). Himalayan information subject gateway in digital era: A proposal for its development. *DESIDOC Journal of Library & Information Technology*, 23(2), 3-9. doi: 10.14429/dbit.23.2.3593

53. Krishnamurthy, M. (2005, July). Designing a gateway interface: Conceptual frame work for library and information science. *Information Studies*, 11(3), 195-204.

54. Mahemei, L. K., Thulasi, K., & Rajashekar, T.B. (2005). Approaches to taxonomy development: Some experiences in the context of an academic institute information portal. In: *International conference on information management in a knowledge society*, 21-25 February, 2005, Mumbai, India,(pp. 315-326.) Retrieved from http://eprints.iisc.ac.in/2853/1/icim-paper1.pdf accessed on 04.05.2020

55. MasoomRaza, M., & Eqbal, M. (2005). Design and development of library and information science gateway: An Indian initiative. *International Information & Library Review*, 37(4), 365-374. doi: 10.1080/10572317.2005.10762694

56. Lalhmachhuana. (2006, November). Subject information gateways as the scholars' pathways for avoiding the internet chaos: New prospects and challenges for LIS professionals. In Manoj Kumar K. (Eds.), *4th Convention planner-2006: Digital preservation, management, and access to information in the twenty first century*, Mizoram University, Aizawl (pp.418-429). Ahmedabad: INFLIBNET Centre. Retrieved from http://ir.inflibnet.ac.in:8080/ir/ViewerJS/#../bitstream/1944/1324/1/418-429.pdf accessed on 04.05.2020

57. Vijayakumar, M., & Ganesan, A. (2006). Collaborative and interoperable subject gateways. *Information Studies*, 12(4), 213-218.

58. Madhusudhan, M. (2007). Internet use by research scholars in University of Delhi, India. *Library Hi Tech News*, 24(8), 36-42. doi: 10.1108/07419050710836036

59. Gul, S. (2009). *Development of web resources in select fields of social sciences with a view to design a model subject gateway* (Doctoral dissertation, University of Kashmir).

60. Munshi, U. M. (2009). Building subject gateway in a shifting digital world. *DESIDOC Journal of Library & Information Technology, 29*(2), 7-14.

61. Neelakandan, B., Malatesh, N., Surulinathi, M., & Srinivasa, R. (2010). Designing and hosting of biotechnology gateway. *International Journal of Environmental Sciences, 1*(2), 163-175. Retrieved from *http://14.139.186.108/jspui/bitstream/123456789/4977/1/EIJES1016.pdf* accessed on 04.05.2020

62. Rajashekara, G. R. (2010). BT-gate: A subject gateway of biotechnology. *SRELS Journal of Information Management, 47*(4), 427-436. doi: 10.17821/srels/2010/v47i4/44967

63. Kumar, S., & Singh, M. (2011). Access and use of electronic information resources by scientists of national physical laboratory in India: A case study. *Singapore Journal of Library and Information Management, 40*, 33-49. Retrieved from *https://www.researchgate.net/profile/Shailendra_Kumar12/publication/230881125_Access_and_use_of_electronic_information_resources_by_scientists_of_National_Physical_Laboratory_in_India_A_case_study/links/0fcfd505ae3f8b352b000000.pdf* accessed on 05.05.2020

64. Pommi, S. (2011). *Developing a gateway for world digital libraries: A study* (Masters dissertation, Bharathidasan University).

65. Meera, B. M., & Ummer, R. (2012). Online reference zone: A gateway to reference resources in science and technology. *SRELS Journal of Information Management, 49*(1), 55-62. doi: 10.17821/srels/2012/v49i1/43816

66. Sureshkumar, S. (2012). *Design and development of a physics subject gateway at Bharathidasan university library* (Masters dissertation, Bharathidasan University).

67. Bhardwaj, R. K. (2013). Leveraging access to e-resources through gateway: A case study at St. Stephen's College, Delhi. *DESIDOC Journal of Library & Information Technology, 33*(5), 418-425. Retrieved from *https://www.researchgate.net/profile/Raj_Bhardwaj/publication/270492284_Leveraging_Access_to_E-resources_through_Gateway_A_Case_Study_at_St_Stephen's_College_Delhi/links/55ea98fa08ae21d099c45840.pdf* accessed on 05.05.2020

68. Kanetkar, J. (2014). Development of subject gateways: A status update. *DESIDOC Journal of Library & Information Technology, 34*(5). 367-375. doi: 10.14429/djlit.34.5807

69. Manivel, D. (2014). *Design and development of physics gateway: with special reference to Bharathidasan university* (Master's dissertation, Bharathidasan University). Retrieved from *http://14.139.186.108/ jspui/bitstream/123456789/14829/2/manivel%20final%20project1.pdf* accessed on 05.05.2020

70. Thirupathi, J. (2014). *Designing the subject gateway for mathematics and statistics using Webnode* (Doctoral dissertation, Bharathidasan University). Retrieved from *http://14.139.186.108/jspui/bitstream/ 123456789/14831/2/thirupathi.pdf* accessed on 05.05.2020

71. Vijayaselvi, P., & Natarajan, N. O. (2014). A study on the design, development and hosting portal subject gateway of mathematics. *Journal of Advances in Library and Information Science, 3*(3), 275-277. Retrieved from *http://www.jalis.in/pdf/pdf3-3/Vijaya.pdf* accessed on 05.05.2020

72. Yuvaraja, R. (2014). *Design and development of subject gateway with special reference to chemistry* (Masters Dissertation, Bharathidasan University). Retrieved from *http://14.139.186.108/jspui/bitstream/ 123456789/14830/2/R.Yuvaraja%20%202.pdf* accessed on 05.05.2020

73. Singh, A., & Gautam, J. N. (2003). Himalayan information subject gateway in digital era: A proposal for its development. *DESIDOC Journal of Library & Information Technology, 23*(2), 3-9. doi: 10.14429/ dbit.23.2.3593

74. Mahemei, L. K., Thulasi, K., & Rajashekar, T.B. (2005). Approaches to taxonomy development: Some experiences in the context of an academic institute information portal. In *International conference on information management in a knowledge society*, 21-25 February, 2005, Mumbai, India, (pp. 315-326.) Retrieved from *http:// eprints.iisc.ernet.in/2853/1/icimpaper1.pdf* accessed on

75. Vijayakumar, M., & Ganesan, A. (2006). Collaborative and interoperable subject gateways. *Information Studies, 12*(4), 213-218.

76. Madhusudhan, M. (2007).Internet use by research scholars in University of Delhi, India., *Library Hi Tech News, 24*(8), 36-42.doi:10.1108/07419050710836036

77. Munshi, U. M. (2009). Building subject gateway in a shifting digital world. *DESIDOC Journal of Library & Information Technology, 29*(2),7-14.

78. Kumar, S., & Singh, M. (2011). Access and use of electronic information resources by scientists of national physical laboratory in India: A case study. *Singapore Journal of Library and Information Management, 40*, 33-49. Retrieved from *https://www.researchgate.net/ profile/Shailendra_Kumar12/publication/230881125_Access_and_use_*

of_electronic_information_resources_by_scientists_of_National_Physical_Laboratory_in_India_A_case_study/links/0fcfd505ae3f8b352b000000.pdf accessed on 06.05.2020

79. Bhardwaj, R. K. (2013). Leveraging access to e-resources through gateway: A case study at St. Stephen's College, Delhi. *DESIDOC Journal of Library & Information Technology, 33*(5), 418-425. Retrieved from *https://www.researchgate.net/profile/Raj_Bhardwaj/publication/270492284_Leveraging_Access_to_E-resources_through_Gateway_A_Case_Study_at_St_Stephen's_College_Delhi/links/55ea98fa08ae21d099c45840.pdf* accessed on 06.05.2020

80. Kanetkar, J. (2014). Development of subject gateways: A status update. *DESIDOC Journal of Library & Information Technology, 34*(5). 367-375. doi: 10.14429/djlit.34.5807

81. Niyogi, B. (1993). *Information needs in jute and allied fibre industries in India* (Doctoral dissertation, Jadavpur University).

82. Mukhopadhyay, C. (1996). *Documentation in jute technology: Its origin and development* (Doctoral dissertation, University of Calcutta).

83. Banik, M. (2001). *Information services for jute research institutes in Bangladesh: a critical study of the present scenario and a plan for future development* (Doctoral dissertation, Jadavpur University).

84. Niyogi, B. (1993). *Information needs in jute and allied fibre industries in India* (Doctoral dissertation, Jadavpur University).

85. Mukhopadhyay, C. (1996). *Documentation in jute technology: Its origin and development* (Doctoral dissertation, University of Calcutta).

86. Banik, M. (2001). *Information services for jute research institutes in Bangladesh: a critical study of the present scenario and a plan for future development* (Doctoral dissertation, Jadavpur University).

87. Koch, T. (2000). Quality-controlled subject gateways: definitions, typologies, empirical overview. *Online Information Review, 24*(1), 24-34. doi: 10.1108/14684520010320040

88. Robinson, L. & Bawden, D. (1999). Internet subject gateways. *International Journal of Information Management, 19*(6), 511-522. Retrieved from *http://openaccess.city.ac.uk/3184/1/Internet%20subject%20gateways.pdf* accessed on 06.05.2020

89. Bawden, D., & Robinson, L. (2002). Internet subject gateways revisited. *International Journal of Information Management, 22*(2), 157-162. doi: 10.1016/S0268-4012(01)00051-2

90. Kanetkar, J. (2014). Development of subject gateways: A status update. *DESIDOC Journal of Library & Information Technology, 34*(5). 367-375. doi: 10.14429/djlit.34.5807

5
Characteristics of Subject Gateways

- Provide quality information dedicated to selective subject area
- Pre-defined quality controlled methods followed in terms of content creation and selection by subject experts for a particular gateway **(Sladen & Spence, 2000)**[1]
- Information contain in subject gateways are regularly updated by skilled manpower mostly subject experts
- Information contain in subject gateways are organised by information experts, mostly library professionals for better retrieval and dissemination of information **(Ward, 2001)**[2] **(Freshwater, 2002)**[3]
- Provide human assisted rapid information navigation and precision retrieval **(Sreenivasulu, 2000)**[4]
- Search results contain more precision and less recall than conventional search engines or web directories
- Single-window access to all web-based resources **(Sladen & Spence, 2000)**[5]
- Gateways are available on 24×7×365 to information seekers

- Now-a-days different Web2.0 features have been incorporated into the subject gateways for making it more interactive with the information seekers.
- Most of the modern subject gateways provide federated search facility to its user by making the contents compliant with OAI-PMH.
- In order to reach the information seekers of different language, multi-lingual contents, machine translation, multilingual search facility have been introduced in different subject gateways.
- Unlike first-generation subject gateways, today's gateways can be built and maintained by single institution or individual through open source software and content management system.
- Subject gateways provide the facility of classifying web documents on any particular subject through the usage of Floksonomy

REFERENCE

1. Sladen, C. & Spence, M. (2000). Hand picked for quality – a reflection on biz/ed. *Library Consortium Management*, 2(2), 35-43.
2. Ward, D. (2001). Internet resource cataloging: the SUNY Buffalo Libraries' response. *OCLC Systems & Services*, 17(1), 19-26.
3. Freshwater, M. (2002). *Subject gateways: an investigation into their role in the information environment (with particular reference to AERADE, the subject gateway for aerospace and defence*. (Masters Dissertation, University of Central England, 2002). Retrieved from http://citeseerx.ist.psu.edu/viewdoc/download?doi=10.1.1.202.5134&rep=rep1 &type=pdf accessed on 07.04.2020
4. Sreenivasulu, V. (2000). The role of a digital librarian in the management of digital information systems. *The Electronic Llibrary*, 18(1), 12-20. Retrieved from http://eprints.rclis.org/6502/1/role-DL-DIS.pdf accessed on 07.05.2020
5. Sladen, C. & Spence, M. (2000). Hand picked for quality – a reflection on biz/ed. *Library Consortium Management*, 2(2), 35-43.

Development of Subject Gateways Across the Ages

Details of some of the illustrative subject gateways (164 Nos.) are given in the following table: Representative list of Subject Gateways crawled by the "Wayback Machine – The Internet Archive" (http://archive.org/web/) as on 31.03.2020

Year of First Crawl	Name of Subject Gateway and its Web-address	Subjects Covered	Features (As described in the respective websites archived in the Internet Archive)	Originator	Year of Existence	Active/ Closed
1996	IPL: Information You Can Trust http://www.ipl.org Formerly: Internet Public Library (ipl2): Information you can trust (2009-2015) http://www.ipl.org Formerly:	Multi-Subject	1. Comprehensive search features 2. Provides online reference service 3. Consists of a youth division known as 'KidSpace' 4. Consists of a Teen division called 'TeenSpace' 5. Consists of Blogs collection	Student Brands, LLC Formerly: Drexel University Formerly: University of Michigan,	24	Active [Closed on 30th June 2015, again Re-opened on January 2020]

Year	Name	Subject	Owner	Status
	Internet Public Library: (1995-2008)		School of Information	Closed on 2014
	6. Consists of Web Technologies Collection 7. Consists of a collection for Deaf people 8. It is a public service organization			18
1996	Art, Design, Architecture and Media (ADAM) Gateway http://adam.ac.uk/	Art, Design, Architecture & Media	ADAM Consortium Partners (Academic Institutions)	Closed on 2007
	1. Free online services 2. Best web resources selected by subject experts 3. Keyword searching and browsing facility			11
1996	Biz/ed: Business education on the Internet http://bized.ac.uk/	Business, Management and Economics	University of Bristol	
	1. Had a unique combination of primary and secondary teaching and learning resources 2. High degree of topicality and currency 3. Integration of Web-based materials 4. Deep appreciation of the learning process. 5. Recognition of the different ways in which people learn. 6. Creation of resources which appeal to a range of learning styles			

Year	Name	Subject	Features	Provider	No.	Status
1996	ChemWeb: Central to science *http://www.chemweb.com/* Formerly: ChemWeb: The World Wide Club for the Chemical Community	Chemistry	1. Provides information to chemists for R&D, product development and self-development 2. Provides access to abstracts, papers, journals, books, conferences news, forums 3. Provides access to databases which offer structure-based searching	Chemindustry.com Inc. Formerly: ChemWeb Inc.	24	Active
1996	ARGUS Clearing House: *The Premier Internet Research Library* *http://www.clearinghouse.net/*	Arts, Humanities, Media & Social Sciences, etc.	Provides a single-window access point for topical guides on different subjects. These guides will help to identify, describe, and evaluate Internet-based information resources.	Argus Associates, Inc.	9	Closed on 2005
1996	EdNA:Education Network Australia (1996-2011) *http://www.edna.edu.au/*	Education	1. Support and promote the benefits of the Internet for learning, education and training in Australia 2. Organized around Australian curriculum 3. Tools are free to Australian educators	Commonwealth of Australia	15	Closed on 30th September 2011

44 *Information Organization & Dissemination Through Subject Gateways*

Development of Subject Gateways Across the Ages 45

| 1996 | HDS: History Data Service http://hds.essex.ac.uk | History | 1. Collects, preserves, and promotes the use of digital resources
2. Support historical research, learning and teaching
3. Provides access and support for a range of historical datasets
4. Preserves deposited data collections for long duration
5. Offers online guidance on creating and documenting digital resources from historical sources
6. Has dedicated help desk and web site
7. Regularly updates web-based FAQs | University of Essex | 24 | Active |
| 1996 | Iowa State | Entomo- | 1. Provides innovative and | John Van Dyk | 24 | Active |

		logy	practical solutions to insect-based challenges in public health and agriculture	of Iowa State University, Department
Entomology Index of Internet resources http://www.ent. iastate.edu/List/	1996		2. Provides teaching, research, of Entomology and extension services
3. Provides information on basic and applied entomology
4. Helps to discover new knowledge/relationships that provides novel solutions to emerging and future problems
5. Strong relationships with collaborators, public agencies and private industry
6. Gateway uses of web-based delivery/outreach	
Multimedia Authoring Web http://www.mcli. dist.maricopa.edu/ authoring/		Multimedia1. Helps programming by non-programmers
2. This gateway is a resource collection of pointers to Internet sites (MCLI)
3. Updated from manually		Maricopa Center for Learning and Instruction (MCLI)	10	Closed On March 23, 2006

Development of Subject Gateways Across the Ages

| 1996 | OMNI - Organizing Medical Networked Information (renamed BIOME and later changed to Intute which was closed on July, 2011, details of project can be found in UK Web Archive) http://www.omni.ac.uk/ | Clinical research, Health and Medicine | 1. It is a free gateway to evaluated high quality internet resources in Health and Medicine
2. Aimed at students, researchers, academics and practitioners in the health and medical sciences
3. Created by a core team of information specialists and subject experts based at the University of Nottingham Greenfield Medical Library
4. Apart from multimedia it also includes web development resources maintained set of resource links to a dynamic, searchable database | Joint Information Systems Committee (JISC). (UK Higher Education) Formerly: OMNI Consortium | 15 | Closed on July, 2011 |
| 1996 | Poly-Cy: Internet Resources for Political Science http://www.polsci.wvu.edu/PolyCy/ | Political Science | 1. Contains a directory of websites on political science
2. Topics include International Affairs, Public Policy, and Public Affairs etc. | Bob Duval, Dept. of Political Science, West Virginia University | 11 | Closed on 6th January, 2007 |

47

Year	Name of Subject Gateway	Subject Covered	Features	Funded/Sponsored by	No. of Resources	Status
1996	Dialog Solutions http://www.dialog.com/ Erstwhile: The Dialog Corporation Erstwhile: Knight-Ridder Information Web Site	Social Science	1. Empowering researchers and librarians around the world 2. Innovative information content and technologies 3. Preserves rich, vast and varied information 4. Uses digital technologies that enhance its discovery, sharing and management 5. Provides services that enable strategic acquisition, management and discovery of information collections	ProQuest LLC Formerly: The Dialog Corporation plc Formerly: Knight-Ridder Information, Inc.	24	Active
1996	Social Science Information Gateway (SOSIG) http://www.sosig.ac.uk/	Social Sciences	1. Freely available internet services which provide a trusted source of selected, high quality Internet information for researchers and practitioners in the social sciences, business and law 2. It was a part of the UK Resource Discovery Network(RDN) 3. SOSIG Internet Catalogue	Joint Information Systems Committee (JISC), (UK Higher Education) Formerly: Economics and Social Research Council (ESRC)	13	Closed on July 2011

| 1996 | A Sociological Tour through Cyberspace http://faculty.trinity.edu/mkearl/ | Sociology | 1. Contains general sociological resources on Sociological theory
2. Contains data resources and some useful web tools
3. Contains research methods and statistics
4. Guides to write a research paper
5. Search-engines helps in subject based inquiries was an online database of high quality internet resources
4. Contains Social Science Search Engine | Michael C. Kearl, Department of Sociology & Anthropology Trinity University San Antonio, Texas | 12 | Closed on May 2008 |
| 1997 | Agriculture Network Information Collaborative: A Knowledge Discovery System for Agriculture http://www.agnic.org/ Formerly : Agriculture Network Information Centre | Agri-culture | 1. 'AgNIC' is a voluntary alliance of members
2. Members seeking agricultural information over the internet are dedicated to enhancing collective information and services among themselves | Agriculture Network Information Centre | 23 | Active |

Development of Subject Gateways Across the Ages 49

| 1997 | Arts and Humanities Data Service (AHDS) http://www.ahds.ac.uk/ | Arts & Humanities | 1. Contains substantial collection of electronic texts, databases, images, and mixed media resources
2. Provides referral information about similar resources
3. Free or at-cost access to all services for the Higher and Further education communities
4. Full-text and web-based resources
5. Committed to the identification, delivery and preservation of reliable, freely-available, evaluated, digital content and quality services for agriculture, food, and natural resources information
3. Provides increasing access to information and expertise | King's College London, Library Arts & Humanities Research Council And Joint Information Systems Committee (JISC) | 12 | Closed on April 2009 |

| 1997 | BUBL Link: Catalogue of Internet Resources http://bubl.ac.uk/link | Multi-Subject | 1. Selected Internet resources covering all academic subject areas
2. Search by Title, Author, Description, and Subject Terms
3. All items are selected, evaluated, catalogued and described
4. Resources are catalogued according to DDC (Dewey Decimal Classification)
5. Subject terms are based on LCSH subject headings
4. Expert guidance on the creation and scholarly use of digital materials
5. Provides professional cataloguing and documentation services
6. Provides expert information on resource availability and usefulness | BUBL Information Service, Andersonian Library, Strathclyde University | 16 | Closed |

Year	Name	Subject	Description	Host		Status
1997	Conflict Archive on the Internet (CAIN) http://cain.ulst.ac.uk/	Conflict Studies	1. Contains information and source material on 'the Troubles' and politics in Northern Ireland from 1968 to the present. 2. It also having some material on society and politics in the region 3. It has searchable bibliographies and databases 4. Intended for first-time users or anyone who is having problems finding information 6. Links are checked and fixed each month 7. National information service for the higher education community	University of Ulster, Queen's University of Belfast and the Linen Hall Library, Belfast	23	Active
1997	Cyburbia : The Urban Planning portal http://cyburbia.ap.buffalo.edu/pairc/ Formerly: PAIRC - The Planning and	Planning & Urbanism	1. Contains a comprehensive directory of Internet resources relevant to planning, architecture, urbanism 2. Contains information about	Dan Tasman Buffalo School of Architecture and Planning, Department of Planning	5	Closed

Development of Subject Gateways Across the Ages 53

	Architecture Internet Resource Center http://www.arch.buffalo.edu/pairc/		architecture and planning related mailing lists and Usenet newsgroups 3. Having Message Boards and Discussion Areas for different forums		
1997	Design Library http://www.dh.umu.se/design_lib/design_library.html	Industrial Design, Interaction Design, Graphic Design, Environmental Design & Design Schools.	1. The gateway deals with different aspects of design 2. The site is divided into various sub-topics 3. Each topic will contain relevant information both academic and commercial, as well as mailing lists	Institute of Design, Umeå University, Sweden	5 Closed
1997	Deutscher Bildungs-Server (Teaching materials and projects online) http://dbs.schule.de/db/listen.html Now https://www.bildungsserver.de/onlineressourcen.html	German Education System	1. Provides information on German and worldwide Education system 2. Provides access to high-quality information and Internet sources - fast, up-to-date, comprehensive and free of charge 3. It refers primarily to Internet resources	DBS	23 Active

| 1997 | Edinburgh Engineering Virtual Library (EEVL) http://www.eevl.ac.uk/ | Engineering | 1. The UK gateway to networked engineering information on the Internet
2. Provides high quality information resources in Engineering for the UK higher education and research community
3. World-Wide-Web interface to a catalogue of Engineering information resources available on the Internet
4. Resources are selected, catalogued, classified and subject-indexed by experts to ensure that only current, high-quality or useful resources are included
5. It has a EEVL E-Journal Search Engine (EESE)
6. EEVL offered Xtra Cross Search Service
7. Facilitated one step jobs search
8. Provided information on Recent Advances In Engineering (RAM) | Joint Information Systems Committee (JISC) (UK Higher Education) | 14 | Closed (Renamed Intute which was closed on July, 2011, details of project can be found in UK Web Archive). Most of the services incorporated in TechXtra |

| 1997 | Edward Lowe Foundation http://www.lowe.org/smbiznet/sites/index.htm | Business and Economics | 1. 'Business Builders' for step-by-step interactive modules on all aspects of starting and growing a business
2. 'Interactive Toolbox' for self-calculating financial management and assessment tools
3. 'Business Resources' for links, news, facts and information
4. 'Interactive Forum' for get in touch with other experts and entrepreneurs who can provide advice, exchange ideas or simply lend moral support. | Edward Lowe Foundation | 2 | Closed |
| 1997 | Energy Information on the Internet (EII) http://www.ecn.nl/eii/main.html | Energy | 1. Provides energy-related information sources that can be accessed through Internet
2. Energy information on internet are described and characterized in a special format | Netherlands Energy Research Foundation ECN | 21 | Closed |

Year	Name & URL	Subject	Description	Affiliation	No.	Status
			3. Helps energy experts in qualitative selection of energy information			
1997	Europeana Collections (2020 - onwards) https://www.europeana.eu/portal/en Formerly: The European Library: Connecting knowledge (2012-2019) http://www.theeuropeanlibrary.org/tel4/ Formerly: Gabriel (Gateway and Bridge to Europe's National Libraries) http://portico.bl.uk/gabriel/en/welcome.html	Multi-Subject	1. Designed to meet the needs of the research community worldwide 2. Offers quick and easy access to the collections of the 48 National Libraries of Europe and leading European Research Libraries 3. Users can cross-search and reuse digital items and bibliographic records	European Union Formerly: The European Library	23	Active
1997	Healio http://www.healio.com Formerly: Medical Matrix http://www.medmatrix.org/	Clinical Medicine	1. Health information meant for health care specialists 2. Selects and customize Disseminates healthcare news for daily practice of medicine	Healio Formerly: Healhtel Corporation	23	Active

| 1997 | Health on the Net (HON) http://www.hon.ch | Medicine and Healthcare | Health On The Net Foundation | 23 | Active |

3. Designed as an in-depth specialty clinical information website
4. Offers best news reporting, dynamic multimedia, question-and-answer columns etc.

1. Helps in the development and application of new information technologies, notably in the fields of health and medicine
2. Promotes and guides the deployment of useful and reliable online health information, and its appropriate and efficient use
3. HON is a Non-profit, non-governmental organization, accredited to the Economic and Social Council of the United Nations
4. 'HONcode' certification is

| 1997 | iLove Languages: Your guide to languages on the Web (2001 onward) http://www.ilovelanguages.com/ Formerly: The Human-Languages Page http://www.june29.com/HLP | Languages | 1. A comprehensive catalogue of language-related Internet resources
2. Offers online language lessons, translating dictionaries, native literature, translation services, software, language schools, or just a little information on a language
3. Provides best 2400 language links of the Web | Tyler Jones Formerly: Tyler Chambers | 23 | Active |

5. 'HONsearch' is used for searching only reliable and trustworthy medical websites
6. 'HONtools' is a free services to enhance and improve online experience
7. 'HONtopics' provides access to a varied list of reliable medical/health topics

used for improving the quality of online health information

| 1997 | Internet Library for Librarians http://www.itcompany.com/inforetriever | Information Resources for Librarians | 1. Provides a one-stop shopping centre for librarians to locate Internet resources related to their profession
2. Table of contents broadly divided into three parts (Ready reference, librarianship and Accessories etc.) | Created by: Vianne Tang Sha and Published by: InfoWorks Technology Company | 23 | Active |
| 1997 | Philosophy Around The Web http://users.ox.ac.uk/~worc0337/phil_index.html | Philosophy Studies | 1. Acts as a guide and a gateway to philosophy resources on the Internet
2. Contains a simplified index of the contents of the site
3. Philosophical resources and indices organized into topics
4. Provides links to Print and Online journals on Philosophy
5. Provides reference resources on Philosophy
6. Contains a Discussion | Dr. Peter J. King of University of Oxford, UK | 23 | Active |

| 1997 | Population Index on the Web http://popindex.princeton.edu/index.html | Political Science | 1. Index covers all fields of interest to demographers, including fertility, mortality, population size and growth, migration, nuptiality and the family, research methodology, projections and predictions, historical demography, and demographic and economic interrelations
2. Input is derived from original publications including monographs, journal articles, other serial publications, working papers, doctoral dissertations, machine- | Office of Population Research, Princeton University | 23 | Active |

Forum, Information conferences and seminars, Information on Jobs and provides a directory of Philosophers

| 1997 | Psychology.org
http://www.psychology.org/
Formerly:
Encyclopedia of Psychology
Formerly:
The Psychology Gateway | Psychology | 1. Intended to facilitate browsing in any area of psychology
2. Information generated by respected researchers and practitioners of psychology
3. It has hierarchical database of links to websites
4. Provides information about scientific psychology
5. Offers centralized online psychology resources and publish original innovative psychology scholarship | readable data files, and relevant acquisitions lists and bibliographies.
3. Selection of citations is based on the quality and relevance of the material
4. This website also provides a search interface to the entire Population Index database for 1986–2000, a total of 46,035 citations | Individual Dr. William Palya Department of Psychology, Lafayette College | 23 | Active |

1997	Research Resources for the Social Science http://socsciresearch.com/	Social Science	1. Provides a single gateway to research resources for the Social Science 2. It is divided into different sections 3. Several information links along with contents are given as per specified sections	McGraw-Hill Ryerson Limited	21	Closed
1997	SciCentral: Gateway to the best science news sources http://www.scicentral.com	All Scientific Disciplines	1. Science aggregator of breaking research news from the most reputable and reliable sources 2. It is the trusted source of information (Reference Source) other websites 3. Sources are hand-picked and ranked based on seven criteria (i.e. Reliability, Timeliness of the information, Extent of daily coverage, Multidisciplinary coverage, Leads to follow up information, and Presentation and general appeal	SciLink, Inc.	23	Active

| 1997 | SocioSite
http://www.pscw.uva.nl/sociosite/TOPICS/index.html | Social Science | 1. Provides access to information and resources relevant for sociologists and other social scientists
2. Provides a comprehensive listing of all sociology resources on the Internet
4. Contents freely accessible to online readers are only considered for this gateway | Albert Benschop of Sociology Department, University of Amsterdam | 14 | Closed |
| 1997 | World Wide Art Resources
http://wwar.com/ | Arts | 1. Provides art, art services and art information to millions of clients, artists, buyers, advertisers, news media, educators and students
2. Provides Artist/Premiere portfolio services to emerging and established artists
3. Distribute weekly international art information to its thousands of subscribers | World Wide Arts Resources, Corp. | 23 | Active |

1997	www.plastics.com Formerly: Polymers DotCom	Plastics and Polymers	1. Index all web sites pertaining to plastics and polymers 2. Describes and categorize the links accurately 3. Providing content and services designed to engage, inform and educate plastics professionals.	Plastics, Agency LLC Formerly: World WideWeb Labs	23	Active
1998	A Reasoned Index to Political Philosophy http://lgxserver.uniba.it /lei/filpol/filpole/homefpe.htm	Political Science	1. Organizes the reasoned index for the political problems of philosophy 2. Helps philosophers in answering political questions 3. Scholars can propose or update links	Maria Chiara Pievatolo University of Pisa, Italy	17	Closed
1998	Academic Info http://www.academicinfo.net/index.html	Multi-Subject	1. Subject area specific authoritative educational internet resources 2. Aims to cover all aspects of education 3. Brings information about the best educational	Librarian Michael Madin	22	Active

1998	Age Info - Worldwide Resources in Ageing *http://www.cpa.org.uk/ageinfo/worldres.html*	Social Work	1. Information service about old age and ageing 2. Provides worldwide resources on aging Provides bibliographic database on ageing 3. Directory of organizations active in the field of old age and ageing 4. Provides international calendar of events, listing courses, conferences, meetings, training sessions and other events going to take place in the field of ageing and old age institutions and programs for current and aspiring students	Centre for Policy on Ageing	22 Active
1998	Artchive *http://www.artchive.com/ftp_site.htm*	Art Links to art movements, artists and images	1. Images, text and articles of this site are for private, non-profit use only 2. Images are made available for educational purposes 3. Sources are updated regularly	Individual Mark Harden	22 Active

| 1998 | BioMedNet
http://www.bmn.com/ | Life-Sciences | 1. It is a website for life science researchers
2. Membership is free, and members can search all of 'BioMedNet' without charges
3. Full text access to the Trends and Current Opinion titles is available through subscription. | Elsevier | 6 | Closed |
| 1998 | British Academy Portal
http://www.britac.ac.uk/ | Humanities & Social Science | 1. Supports the humanities and social sciences in the UK and beyond
2. Provides leadership in representing the interests of research and learning nationally and internationally
3. Supports research of the highest quality
4. Communicate and disseminate new knowledge and ideas
5. Promotes international research links and collaborations | The British Academy | 22 | Active |

| 1998 | CFD Online http://www.cfd-online.com/ | Fluid Dynamics | 1. It is an online centre for Computational Fluid Dynamics
2. Contains several discussion forums, a jobs database, a free CFD reference in the form of a CFD-Wiki, a news and announcement forum, a books guide, an events calendar, and a comprehensive annotated link section with pointers to CFD resources around the world
3. Offer high-quality web services to the CFD community
4. Site is independent and self-financed | CFD-Online | 22 | Active |
| 1998 | DataZone http://www.epinet.org/datazone/ | Statistics | 1. Provides national, state and regional level statistical data related to Economics
2. Provides detailed quarterly | The Economic Policy Institute | 14 | Closed |

| 1998 | Dutch Electronic Subject Service (DutchESS) http://www.konbib.nl/dutchess/ | Multi-Subject | 1. It is a directory service of academic internet resources
2. Provides access to a collection of resources relevant to academic research, via a bilingual interface (English and Dutch)
3. Resources were selected by subject specialist as per selection policy
4. Resources were classified according to the Dutch Basic Classification scheme
5. Abstract of the resources were also provided in English | Koninklijke Bibliotheek (the National Library of the Netherlands) | 9 | Closed |
| 1998 | EnviroLink: the online environmental community http://library.envirolink.org/ | Environ-ment | 1. It is a non-profit o online community
2. Provides comprehensive, | The EnviroLink Network | 19 | Closed |

Development of Subject Gateways Across the Ages

Year	Name	Subject	Description	Provider	Count	Status
1998	InfoLaw http://www.infolaw.co.uk/	Law	1. Leading legal web gateway in UK 2. Produces legal resources catalogue 3. Publishes the Internet Newsletter for Lawyers 4. Provides publishing, social media and advertising services to the legal sector 5. Provides free internet services to non-profit organizations of the environmental and animal rights communities 4. Acts as a clearinghouse on the Internet for the environmental community 3. Promotes a sustainable society by connecting individuals and organizations up-to-date environmental information and news	Information for Lawyers Limited	22	Active
1998	INFOMINE: Scholarly Internet Resource	Multi-Subject	1. It is a virtual library of Internet resources for	University of California	16	Closed

Collections http://infomine.ucr.edu/Main.html	1998	(General, including, Arts, Humanities & Social Sciences)	university level users 2. Contains useful Internet resources (i.e. databases, electronic journals, electronic books, bulletin boards, mailing lists, online library card catalogues, articles, directories of researchers, etc.)	Riverside Library
Internet Directory for Botany http://www.botany.net/IDB/	1998	Botany and Ecology	1. It is an index to botanical information available on the Internet 2. Consists of a search engine	Harvard University Herbarium, University of Helsinki, Botanical Museum, Oakridge	22 Active
LibrarySpot.com http://www.libraryspot.com/		Library and Information Science	1. It is a free virtual library resource centre for valuable research information 2. Brings the best library and reference sites together 3. Sites featured in this gateway are hand-selected and reviewed by editorial team for their quality and contents 4. Designed to make finding	StartSpot Mediaworks, Inc.	22 Active

| 1998 | NOVAGate https://www.nmbu.no/nova Formerly: http://nova-university.org/ | Forestry, Veterinary, Agriculture, Food Sciences and Environmental Sciences | 1. Funded by member institutions promote cooperation between the member institutions in higher education 2. Initiate, administer and information on the internet a quick, easy and enjoyable 3. Provides knowledge in the fields of agriculture, animal sciences, forestry, veterinary medicine, food sciences, environmental sciences, aquaculture and related biosciences 4. Enhance the quality and broaden the scope of teaching | NOVA University Network | 22 | Active |
| 1998 | Oxford Text Archive http://ota.ox.ac.uk/ | Literary and Linguistic Resources | 1. Develops, collects, catalogues and preserves electronic literary and linguistic resources for use in Higher Education, research, teaching and learning | University of Oxford | 22 | Active |

1998	physicsworld.com *http://physicsworld.com* Formerly PhysicsWeb: The websites for physicists *http://physicsweb.org*	Physics	1. Website meant for physicists 2. Disseminate information on all aspects of physics 3. Contains web resources, patent news, book reviews, event calendar etc. 4. Holds thousands of texts in more than 25 different languages	Institute of Physics	22 Active
1998	PICK: Library and Information Science Resources on the Internet *http://www.aber.ac.uk/~tplwww/e/*	Library and Information Science	1. It is a gateway to quality Librarianship and Information Science (LIS) resources on the Internet 2. Holds a research collection of international reputation in LIS 3. Collects and organizes of selected LIS resources	Thomas Parry Library, University of Wales Aberystwyth	9 Closed

2. Advices on the creation and use of linguistic resources
3. Involves in the development of standards and infrastructure for electronic language resources.

| 1998 | Venables Legal Resources http://venables.co.uk/ Formerly: Portal to Legal Resources in the UK and Ireland | Law | 1. Independent legal web sites in the UK and Ireland
2. Provides a comprehensive set of links to useful legal resources
3. Designed to help legal community and also to individuals looking for legal resources
4. Helps the users in their legal problems | Delia Venables | 22 | Active |
| --- | --- | --- | --- | --- | --- | --- |
| 1998 | Preserving Access to Digital Information (PADI) (including ICADS) http://pandora.nla.gov.au/tep/10691 Formerly: http://nla.gov.au/padi | Library & Information Science | 1. Provides information about relevant conferences, meetings and workshops
2. Provides links to reports about projects being undertaken in the field of digital preservation and access
3. Includes a list of glossaries, selected bibliographies, related discussion lists, journals, web sites and organizations
4. Assists all those wishing to preserve access to significant digital information | National Library of Australia | 12 | Closed |

Year	Name & URL	Subject	Features	Developed by	No. of resources	Status
1998	Psych Web http://www.psywww.com/	Psychology	1. Contains lots of psychology-related information for students and teachers of psychology 2. Site can be browse through the subdivisions or keywords 3. Responsive web design makes the site smart phone friendly	Russell A. Dewey	22	Active
1998	SciGate: The IISc Science Information Portal http://www.ncsi.iisc.ernet.in/	Science	1. It is a science information portal and gateway website developed for the academic community of IISc 2. Provides single point access to a variety of locally hosted and Internet-based science, engineering, medicine and management information resources 3. Access to databases and other electronic resources	Indian Institute of Science (IISc), Bangalore	10	Closed

Development of Subject Gateways Across the Ages

1998	Scott's Botanical Links http://www.ou.edu/cas/botany-micro/bot-linx/	Botany	1. Accumulates botanical resources for the educational community 2. Provides botany education resources available in internet 3. Botanical sites are rated on a 4-star scale emphasizing educational value, completeness and scientific correctness 4. Includes subject index and RSS feed 5. Apart from selection of sources from the drop-down lists one can also search using simple and advanced search interfaces	Dr. Scott Russell, Dept. of Botany & Microbiology, Univ. of Oklahoma	22	Active
1998	Scout Report Archive (2002-)	Computer Science	1. Contains best Internet resources chosen by the	The Internet Scout Research Group,	22	Active

licensed to IISc is restricted to IISc users
4. It also provided highly useful scholarly sources on the Internet

		editorial staff of the Scout Report, which have been catalogued and organized for efficient browsing and searching	University of Wisconsin-Madison Formerly: Internet Scout Group	
1998	SSG-FI/ Special Subjects Guides http://www.SUB. Uni-Goettingen.de/ ssgfi/index.html	Multi-Subject	1. There are different Special Subject Guides (i.e. the Geo Guide, the Math Guide and the History Guide, Anglo-American Literature Guide and Forestry Guide) in SSG-FI
2. Scholarly relevant information resources available in the WWW is assessed and indexed in a structured, high-quality format	"Deutsche Forschungs gemeinschaft" (DFG)	15	Closed

https://scout.wisc. edu/archives/
Formerly:
Scout Report Signpost
http://www.signpost. org/signpost/

and Library Resources

2. Designed to guide U.S. higher education to quality electronic resources
3. Resources reviewed are freely available
4. Can be browsed by Subject Headings or by Library of Congress Classification

Development of Subject Gateways Across the Ages

Year	Name	Subject	Description	Developer	No. of resources	Status
1998	The Gateway: performing arts centre of Suffolk County *http://thegateway.org/* Formerly: The Gateway to 21ˢᵗ Century Skills & The Gateway to Educational Materials (GEM)	Education	1. Provides the key to one-stop access to high quality education resources 2. Consortium effort to provide educators with quick and easy access to thousands of educational resources found on different Internet sites 3. Developed a set of widely used standards used for describing educational resources 4. Assess information sources for scholars and include it in specific subject guide 5. Enable users to get an overview of the relevant information sources in specific subject area 3. Bibliographies and data available in printed or CD-ROM format are also integrated into the information guide	The U.S. Department of Education's National Library of Education	22	Active

| 1998 | Physicsworld http://physicsworld.com/ Formerly: The Internet Pilot to Physics (TIPTOP) (Transferred to Institute of Physics Website) http://physicsweb.org/TIPTOP/ | Physics | 1. Information is freely available for the benefit of the worldwide physics community
2. Created to serve everyone interest in science particularly in physics
4. Developed tools to make creating resource descriptions | IOP Publishing Ltd. | 22 | Active |
|---|---|---|---|---|---|---|
| 1998 | World Lecture Hall http://www.utexas.edu/world/lecture/index.html | Multi-Subject | 1. Contains links to pages to be delivered as online course material
2. Provides free online course materials from around the world
3. Pages can be visited by anyone interested in courseware on the Internet | Academic Computing and Instructional Technology Services of Univ. of Texas | 12 | Closed |
| 1998 | WWW Virtual Library http://vlib.org | Multi-Subject (Catalogue of the Web) | 1. Oldest catalogue of the web
2. Run by a loose confederation of volunteers experts in their subject areas | Tim Berners-Lee Later The Council of The WWW Virtual Library | 22 | Active |

1999	About.com http://home.about.com/education/index.htm	Multi-Subject	1. Network of sites led by expert guides 2. Contain site index on different subjects 3. It also has a search engine and a discussion forum 3. Individual indexes are scattered in different servers around the world 4. Central catalogue pages are maintained by the Council of the VL 5. VL also offer various materials for download	About.com, Inc.	15	Closed
1999	AccessToLaw https://www.accesstolaw.com/	Law	1. Provides annotated links to selected legal web sites 2. The site helps the legal practitioner to find legal information over internet 3. Apart from subscription service, most of the linked sites are free 4. Contents are selected, annotated and updated by an experienced team of information professionals	Inner Temple Library, London	21	Active

1999	al-bab: An open door to the Arab world http://www.al-bab.com/arab/comp.htm Formerly: Arab Gateway	Arab	1. Initially intended to be electronic gateway to information about Yemen and later to all Arab states 2. Contains a collection of links to material about Yemen 3. Meant for researchers, students, journalists and anyone else who wanted to know Arab world 4. Provides background information and context	Individual Brian Whitaker	21	Active
1999	Art History Resources on the Web http://witcombe.sbc.edu/ARTHLinks.html	Art History	1. Provides information on different types of Arts over the ages including links and online contents	Individual Christopher L.C.E. Witcombe	21	Active
1999	ChemDex http://www.chemdex.org/	Chemistry	1. The directory of chemistry on the internet 2. Addition and correction can be done interactively 3. Supports facetted search other than keyword search	University of Sheffield, Department of Chemistry.	18	Closed

| 1999 | ChemistryWeb: Internet resources http://www.ssc.ntu.edu.sg:8000/chemweb/html/ | Chemistry | 1. Developed to customize search for chemical information
2. Site is meant for chemistry researchers, educators and students
3. This online guide is compiled to filter useful chemical information and resources on the Internet
4. Contains 'teaching resources' useful for chemistry and science educators and 'selected resources' is useful to users of computing
5. User interface is designed in such a way that helps to navigate very quickly to different parts of the guide | Thiam-Seng KOH | 2 | Closed |
| 1999 | DMOZ: the Open Directory Project http://www.dmoz.org/ | Multi-Subject (Web Directory) | 1. Largest and most comprehensive human-edited directory of the Web
2. Historically known as the Open Directory Project | AOL Inc. | 18 | Closed after 17/03/2017 (Static Mirror site available) |

1999	European IP Helpdesk (2011-2017) https://www.iprhelpdesk.eu/ Formerly IPR Helpdesk (1999-2012) http://www.ipr-helpdesk.org	Intellectual Property Rights	1. Offers free, first-line support on IP matters in Europe 2. Services of the European IPR Helpdesk are delivered and managed by a consortium of three partners 3. This directory is 100% Free 4. Most widely distributed data base of Web content 5. Provides input to the Web's largest and most popular search engines	European Union Formerly European Commission DG Enterprise.	21	Active
1999	MathGuide http://www.mathguide.de/ Formerly: http://www.sub.uni-goettingen.de/ssgfi/math/	Mathematics	1. It is a virtual library of mathematics 2. Helps scientists to find mathematically relevant information 3. Developed by a team of mathematicians and librarians	MathGuide, SUB Göttingen	21	Active
1999	History Guide http://www.sub.uni-goettingen.de/ssgfi/aac-	History	1. Internet-based subject gateway provides scholarly information in history	SSG-FI, SUB Göttingen	15	Closed

Year	Name/URL	Subject	Description	Developed by	No. of records	Status
1999	HUMBUL Humanities Hub (Renamed Intute which was closed on July, 2011, details of project can be found in UK Web Archive) *http://www.humbul.ac.uk/ hist/index.html* Formerly Anglo-American History Guide	Humanities (Archaeology, Classics, History, Language, Literature and Religion)	1. Dedicated to discovering, evaluating and cataloguing online resources in the humanities 2. It facilitates access to its records in variety of ways 3. It is part of the Resource Discovery Network 2. It focuses on focus on Anglo-American history 3. Resources are described and evaluated with Dublin Core metadata set	Joint Information Systems Committee (JISC) (UK Higher Education)	12	Closed
1999	InfoQuest *http://roads.itc.gu.edu.au*	Multi-Subject	1. Developed an Internet Web subject resource gateway to specified subjects 2. The gateway is created and maintained using ROADS software 3. Resource were described and organized under subject headings according to its classification 4. Students from 24 subject	Griffith University and Queensland University of Technology Libraries	5	Closed

Year	Gateway	Subject	Features	Hosted by	No.	Status
1999	Jyväskylä Virtual Library http://www.jyu.fi/library/virtuaalikirjasto/engroads.htm	Multi-Subject	1. It is a database contained in The Finnish Virtual Library 2. Describes internet resources on different subject fields 3. Search can be done through subject type and resource type	Jyväskylä University Library	12	Closed
1999	Philosophy in Cyberspace http://www-personal.monash.edu.au/~dey/phil/	Philosophy	1. Indexes thousands of philosophy resources 2. It is annotated and updated regularly 3. Finds resources in the area of philosophy	Dey Alexander of Monash University	7	Closed
1999	Port http://www.rmg.co.uk/ Formerly: http://www.intute.ac.uk/ Formerly: http://www.port.nmm.ac.uk/	Maritime Studies	1. Information gateway of high quality internet resources on maritime studies 2. Resources have been selected and described by	National Maritime Museum	13	Closed

areas and 12 Librarians from 2 universities participated in the project (Middleton, Edwards, & Collins, 1999)[1]

1999	Resource Discovery Network (RDN) http://www.intute.ac.uk/ Formerly: http://www.rdn.ac.uk/	Multi-Subject (General, including, Humanities and Social Sciences)	1. Provides effective access to high quality Internet resources for the UK learning and research communities 2. Give access to full range of online resource (i.e. bibliographic, documentary and data resources) 3. It is a co-operative network consisting of a central organization and a number of independent service providers 4. It is freely accessible	RDN Centre, King's College, London and The University of Bath.	12	Closed
1999	Voice of the Shuttle http://vos.ucsb.edu/	General, including, Arts, to Humanities	1. Provides global web access to online documents related to Humanities	Alan Liu and a development team of English Department	21	Active

Year	Name & URL	Subject	Features	Owner	Resources	Status
2000	123 Help Me http://www.123helpme.com/	Social Science Humanities & Media Web	1. Free directory of online content 2. Provides a structured and briefly annotated guide to online resources on Humanities 3. Emphasizes on both primary and secondary (or theoretical) resources 4. VoS was rebuilt as a database that serves content dynamically on the Web	123HelpMe.com of University of California, Santa Barbara	20	Active
2000	Aerospace Resources on Internet (AERADE) http://aerade.cranfield.ac.uk/	Aerospace and Defence Resources	1. A collection of quality aerospace and defense online information resources 2. This gateway is a free collection of quality assessed resources 3. Resources are selected,	Cranfield University	20	Active

Development of Subject Gateways Across the Ages 87

2000	AGRIGATE http://www.agrigate.edu.au/	Agri-culture, Forestry, Environment, Food, Science, Horti-culture	1. Agriculture Information Gateway for Australian Researchers 2. Provides both online and offline information resources for Agriculture Research 3. Resources are selected by review process done by specialist librarians and researchers on Agriculture 4. Supports identification and dissemination of high quality research materials 5. It is based on NASA Classification and the Military Science index 4. It is fully searchable and browsable evaluated, regularly monitored and updated by subject specialists	University of Melbourne	6	Closed
2000	Alex Catalogue of Electronic Texts http://www.infomotions.	American and English	1. It is a collection of public domain documents from American and English	Individual Eric Lease Morgan	20	Active

com/alex/		Literature	literature and Western philosophy		
			2. A multi-purpose tool for teaching Philosophy and exploring electronic texts		
			3. Provides value-added access to some of the world's great literature		
			4. Texts on American literature, English literature, or Western philosophy available in the public domain or freely distributed texts are collected, classified and included		
ArchNet *www.archnet.org*	2000	Islamic Architecture, Urban Design and Development	1. Focused on architecture, urbanism, environmental and landscape design, visual culture, and conservation issues related to the Muslim world	MIT School of Architecture and Planning and Aga Khan Trust for Culture	20 Active
			2. Provides ready access to unique visual and textual material to facilitate teaching, scholarship, and professional work		

3	2000	ArtSource http://www.ilpi.com/artsource	Art & Architecture	1. A collection point for networked resources on Art and Architecture 2. Resources around the net as well as original materials submitted by librarians, artists, and art historians, etc. 3. This gateway is selective rather than comprehensive	Interactive Learning Paradigms Inc.	20	Active
	2000	Census and Demographic Data (Mansfield University) http://www.mnsfld.edu/depts/lib/census.html	Social Science, Economics, Census	1. Provides Census and demographic information to the users 2. Offers access to different databases and reference information 3. The gateway also gives miscellaneous demographic information to its users	Mansfield University of Pennsylvania	13	Closed
	2000	Digital Librarian http://www.digital-librarian.com/	Multi-Subject	1. General annotated index of online resources maintained individually	Individual: Margaret Vail Anderson	16	Closed

3. Largest open, online architectural library with a focus on Muslim cultures

| 2000 | ELDIS http://www.eldis.org/ | Develop-ment | 1. The gateway aims to provide best information on development, policy, practice and research
2. It is a network of global network of research organizations and knowledge brokers
3. Provides free access to relevant, up-to-date and diverse research on international development issues
4. Documents are organized as per major development themes and the country or region | Institute of Development Studies | 20 | Active |
| 2000 | Engineering Electronic Library, Sweden (EELS) http://eels.lub.lu.se/ | Engin-eering | 1. Served as a manually indexed subject gateway
2. It was an information system for quality assessed information resources on Engineering
3. Attempted to provide links to evaluated engineering resources mainly to the | Swedish Universities of Technology Libraries | 7 | Closed |

Development of Subject Gateways Across the Ages 91

2000	HISTORY: On Line http://www.history.ac.uk/	History	1. Offers high-quality information resources for the teaching and learning of history 2. Provides details of books and articles, UK university lecturers, UK current and past research, and evaluated links to web sites and on-line resources 3. Information is freely available and can be searched and browsed	Institute of Historical Research	20	Active
2000	MCS http://www.aber.ac.uk/media/Functions/mcs.html	Media, Communication Studies	1. 'Meta-index' to internet-based resources, useful for media and communication 2. British-based gateway intended to both British	Daniel Chandler of University of Wales, Aberystwyth	12	Closed

| 2000 | Media UK
http://directory.mediauk.com/ | Mass Communication, Media | 1. Free independent online media directory
2. It contains links to forums, directory, television, radio, newspaper, newsfeeds, job search and shopping
3. A comprehensive collection of Web resources for the academic study of media and communication scholars in the field and to others who are interested in media in the UK | MediaUK.Com Ltd. | 4 | Closed |
| 2000 | MetaChem
http://metachem.ch.adfa.edu.au/ | Chemistry | 1. Single web-based focal point for accessing all kinds of chemistry information resources
2. Provides links, through library catalogues and document delivery services, to print information
3. Each site has been evaluated, described, classified and indexed
4. Organizes information | University of NSW, ADFA, DSTC Pty Ltd. | 3 | Closed |

2000	psci-com http://psci-com.org.uk/	Science Communication and Society	1. It is gateway to evaluated, quality Internet resources relating to public engagement with science 2. Aims to promote science communication to all kind of audience 3. Provides a calendar of events, a monthly bibliography of relevant articles and new additions to Wellcome Trust Library and a link to the psci-com electronic discussion forum 5. Gateway uses effective combination of Dublin Core and PICS format resources to enable searchers to find relevant information quickly and precisely	The Wellcome Trust	5	Closed
2000	PSIgate (Renamed Intute which was closed on July, 2011, details of project can	Physical Sciences, Astronomy, Chemistry,	1. This gateway aims to provide high quality Internet resources on physical science to all stake	Joint Information Systems Committee (JISC) (UK Higher Education)	11	Closed

Name	Year	Subject	Objectives	Funded by	Partners	Status
be found in UK Web Archive) http://www.psigate.ac.uk/		Earth Sciences, Materials Sciences, Physics, And Science History And Policy	holders of physics 2. Provides an online database of relevant, high quality Internet resources, the Internet Resource Catalogue 3. Resources have been selected by information professionals and subject specialists to ensure relevance and quality			
Renardus http://www.renardus.org/	2000	Multi-Subject	1. Quality-controlled subject gateways aims to improve access to existing Internet-based information services across Europe 2. Provides access to selected, quality resources for the academic and research communities 3. Aims to provide users integrated access through	Information Society Technologies (IST) programme	7	Closed

| 2000 | The Math Forum http://mathforum.org/library/ Formerly: The Internet Mathematics Library http://forum.swarthmore.edu/library/ | Mathematics | 1. Provides mathematics education on internet through interactive services to all stake holders of mathematics
2. Encourages communication throughout the mathematical community
3. Provides math-related web resources more accessible
4. Provides high-quality math and math education content
a single interface to different internet-based distributed services
4. Provides option to "Browse by Subject" through hierarchical trees of topics | The Math Forum | 20 | Active |
| 2000 | Vetgate (Renamed Intute which was closed on July, 2011, details of project can be found in UK Web Archive) http://vetgate.ac.uk/ | Animal Health | 1. Gateway to evaluated, high quality internet resources on animal health
2. Created by a core team of information specialists and subject experts based at the University of Nottingham Greenfield Medical Library | Joint Information Systems Committee (JISC) (UK Higher Education) | 11 | Closed |

2001	ALTIS (Renamed Intute Archive) http://www.altis.ac.uk/	Hospitality, Leisure, Sport, Tourism	1. Provides trusted sources of selected, high quality Internet information in the areas of hospitality, leisure, sport and tourism 2. Created by a core team of information specialists and subject experts of University of Birmingham	Joint Information Systems Committee (JISC) (UK Higher Education)	10	Closed
2001	Biogate http://biogate.lub.lu.se/	Biological Sciences	1. Provides 1000 best links in the biological sciences 2. Facilitates advanced search, robot search and cross search facility	Lunds University, Sweden	1	Closed
2001	BIOME (Previously OMNI and later Renamed as Intute which was closed on July, 2011, details of project can be found in UK Web Archive) http://biome.ac.uk	Health and Life Sciences	1. Provides free access to quality information resources in health and life sciences available on Internet 2. Search-engine directs user to Internet resources that have been hand selected and quality evaluated	Joint Information Systems Committee (JISC) (UK Higher Education)	10	Closed
2001	Bureau of Labor Statistics	Statistics	1. Its mission is to collect, analyze, and disseminate	U.S. Department of Labor	19	Active

Development of Subject Gateways Across the Ages

http://www.bls.gov/home.htm

essential economic information to support public and private decision-making.

2. It serves independently to diverse user communities by providing products and services that are objective, timely, accurate, and relevant.

3. Meets the information needs of a rapidly changing U.S. and global economy by continuously improving its products and services

| 2001 | Council of Professional Associations on Federal Statistics (COPAFS) http://www.copafs.org/ | Statistics | 1. Provides links to the Federal Statistical Agencies
2. Provides information to decision makers that demonstrates the value of federal statistics
3. Provides news, reports on federal statistics and also | The Council of Professional Associations on Federal Statistics | 19 | Active |

| 2001 | EdWeb: Exploring Technology and School Reform http://www.edwebproject.org/ | Educational Reform and Information Technology | 1. Examines the role of the Web in education
2. Helped people learn about the Internet as a learning tool
3. Explores the worlds of educational reform and information technology
4. User can search on-line educational resources, learn about trends in education policy and information infrastructure development around the world | Individual: Andy Carvin | 19 | Active |
| 2001 | Forced Migration Online (FMO): a world of information on human displacement http://forcedmigration.org | Refugee Studies | 1. Provides free access to online information on forced migration
2. Selected materials on this site are available for re-use under a Creative Commons license.
3. Committed to provide access to resources | University of Oxford's Department of International Development | 16 | Closed |

| 2001 | International Economics Network
http://www.international economics.net/index.html | Economics | 1. Offers a collection of selected e-resources on international economics from single location
2. It contains documents on global business and finance, international law, and international development
3. Gathers working papers and other key research papers
4. Collate quality news articles and commentary
5. Disseminate key information and updates on international economics | Jamus Jerome Lim | 19 | Active |
| 2001 | Moving Images Gateway
http://www.bufvc. ac.uk/gateway | Moving Image and Sound Materials | 1. Includes over 1,900 websites relating to moving image and sound materials
2. The gateway is subdivided into over 40 subject areas regardless of whether or not they have access to subscription-based services | British Universities Film & Video Council | 19 | Active |

| 2001 | NMAP (Renamed Intute which was closed on July, 2011, details of project can be found in UK Web Archive) http://www.nmap.ac.uk | Medical Science (Nursing, Midwife and Allied Health Professions) | 1. Free catalogue of selected and evaluated Internet resources in Nursing, Midwifery and the Allied Health Professions
2. Created by a core team of information specialists and subject experts coordinated at the University of Nottingham Greenfield Medical Library
3. Closely integrated with the OMNI gateway | Joint Information Systems Committee (JISC) (UK Higher Education) | 10 | Closed |
| 2001 | Resource for Urban Development and Information (RUDI) https://www.transportxtra.com/rudi/news/ Formerly: http://www.rudi.net/ | Urban Design and Transport Resources | 1. Facilitates knowledge sharing and networking for professionals & academics in urban development
2. Contains updated online materials needed for research, proposal preparation, commissioning | Landor Links Ltd. | 19 | Active |

(continuing from previous page)
3. Brings together websites relate to moving images and sound and their use in higher and further education

| 2001 | Property and Building Directory http://www.propertyand buildingdirectory.co.uk/ Formerly: Sapling.info: Architecture, Planning and Landscape information gateway http://www.sapling.info/ Formerly: http://www.sapling.org.uk/ | Architecture, Planning and Landscape | 1. Sapling is a cross-disciplinary links directory based on the fields of architecture, planning and landscape. Links are organized into nine key themes
2. Linked sites are individually reviewed, rated and judged on the quality content and presentation
3. Promote and recognizes high standards of web design that complement excellent and innovative content
4. Fully available on subscription
projects, fact-checking and general reference
3. Provides professional information services | Individual: Graham Soult | 19 | Active |
| 2001 | ViFaTec http://vifatec.tib.uni- | Engineering | 1. Offers access to selected, advanced sources of | University Library / Technical | 12 | Closed |

				information for engineers 2. Provides parallel search in leading specialist databases, and library catalogues with integrated full-text delivery 3. Offers robot-based search service for engineering-related websites 4. Provides full text access of the electronic documents from server of TIB Hannover and FIZ Karlsruhe	Information Library (UB/TIB) of the University of Hannover
2002	MedHist (Renamed Intute which was closed on July, 2011, details of project can be found in UK Web Archive) http://medhist.ac.uk/	Medical and Allied Sciences	1. Offers free access to a searchable catalogue of Internet sites and evaluated quality Internet resources covering the history of medicine and allied sciences 2. Aimed principally towards academic community in higher education sector 3. Developed and managed by the 'Wellcome Library' for the History and Understanding of Medicine	Joint Information Systems Committee (JISC)(UK Higher Education)	9 Closed

hannover.de

2002	Wales on the Web http://www.waleson theweb.org	Multi-Subject (Welsh Studies)	1. It is a bilingual subject gateway to high quality material of Welsh interest on the World Wide Web 2. Objective of the project is the creation of electronic resources for Welsh Studies 3. Enables researchers in all fields to locate material and examples relevant to Wales	The National Library of Wales	12	Closed
2003	Artifact (Renamed Intute which was closed on July, 2011, details of project can be found in UK Web Archive) http://www.artifact.ac.uk/	Arts and Creative Industries	1. Arts and creative industries gateway of the Resource Discovery Network (RDN) 2. Artifact is an Internet Resource Catalogue (IRC) provides access to a collection of high quality online resources and web sites 3. Artifact is a free service, though for some resources subscription may be required 4. Each site has been chosen by subject specialists for its	Joint Information Systems Committee (JISC)(UK Higher Education)	8	Closed

| 2003 | Best of the Web - Social Sciences
http://botw.org/top/Science/Social_Sciences/ | Social Science | 1. It is a online directory spotlighting the web's premier destinations
2. Sites listed in the directory are examined by our team of editors, and qualified are included
3. Review is done to ensure that all sites are appropriately listed in their most relevant category.
4. All sites included must contain substantive unique content, navigate in a user-friendly manner, relevance to higher education teaching, learning and research in arts and creative industries
5. Each site is then evaluated and catalogued by the Artifact cataloguers along with a description of the site and its key features | Best of the Web | 17 | Active |

| 2003 | BioethicsWeb (Renamed Intute which was closed on July, 2011, details of project can be found in UK Web Archive) http://bioethicsweb.ac.uk | Biomedical Ethics, Including Ethical, Social, Legal And Public Policy | 1. Offers free access to a searchable catalogue of evaluated Internet sites and resources covering biomedical ethics 2. Affiliated to the BIOME life sciences gateway and the Resource Discovery Network (RDN) | Joint Information Systems Committee (JISC) (UK Higher Education) | 8 | Closed contain no broken links or pictures, be up and running 24/7 |
| 2003 | Go-Geo http://www.gogeo.ac.uk | Geospatial Information | 1. The gateway allows the discovery of geographic data and related resources exists within UK tertiary education and beyond 2. Supports geospatial searching by interactive map, grid co-ordinates and place name, as well as keywords 3. The gateway facilitates simultaneous searching across many resources | EDINA/UKDA | 13 | Closed |

2003	NBS Erstwhile: Aecportico http://thenbs.com	Building Construction, Engineering Services and Landscape Design	1. It offers distinctive, innovative specification and information solutions to construction industry professionals	RIBA Enterprises Ltd.	17	Active
2004	Cyber-Infrastructure for Phylogenetic Research (CIPRES) Science Gateway https://www.phylo.org/	Evolutionary biology	1. Provides information on Evolutionary Biology 2. This gateway is a public resource for inference of large phylogenetic trees. It is designed to provide all researchers with access to NSF XSEDE's large computational resources through a simple browser interface.	National Science Foundation (NSF)	16	Active
2004	Library & Information Science Gateway http://www.lisgateway.com	Library and Information Science	1. Contents covered in this gateway serve the academic community 2. Links to various electronic resources available on the Internet related to library and information science	Dr. M. Masoom Raza and Monawwar Eqbal of Dept. of Library Information Science Aligarh Muslim University, Aligarh	16	Active

| 2005 | A Guide to Selected Population Resources on Government Web Sites *http://stokeslib.princeton.edu/popstatsrgv.htm* | Population Resources | 1. Provides links to selected population and related data maintained on government web sites around the world
2. Data is derived from Censuses or national surveys and pages appear in Government websites | Princeton University | 15 | Active |
| 2005 | Careers Guide *http://careers-guide.com* | Career Advice and Job Vacancies | 1. Provide free career advice, training and information on Job vacancies in England, Republic of Ireland, Wales, Scotland and Northern Ireland.
2. Provide information on most popular occupation and the path to attain the same
3. Industry governing bodies and training organizations are given free service to add or update their information
4. Also provides online resources and CV service | Careers-guide.com | 15 | Active |

| 2005 | GESource (Renamed Intute which was closed on July, 2011, details of project can be found in UK Web Archive) http://www.gesource.ac.uk/home.html | Geography & Environment | 1. GESource is a free information gateway for Geography and the Environment
2. Includes a core database of high-quality Internet resources catalogued by subject specialists across a number of disciplines (i.e. the environment, general geography, human geography, physical geography etc.)
3. It also includes current awareness services (jobs, news, conferences), reference materials, and other community features | Joint Information Systems Committee (JISC) (UK Higher Education) | 6 | Closed |
| 2005 | MetaMatters (Australia-based Gateways) http://metabrowser.dtdns.net/dcanz2/mb.aspx | Multi-Subject | 1. Links are proved as a reference to metadata resources in Australia and New Zealand as well as wide ranging subject related links overseas
2. Promotes the use of standards based metadata | Dublin Core Australia & New Zealand and National Library of Australia | 1 | Closed |

Development of Subject Gateways Across the Ages

Year	Name	Subject	Description	Organization	#	Status
2005	Minnesota Library Information Network (MnLINK) http://www.mnlink gateway.org	Multi-Subject	1. MNLINK is a state-wide virtual library that electronically links you to Minnesota's rich library resources 2. Serves as a discovery and interlibrary loan interface for library patrons and staff 3. System provides access to electronic resources that are available to Minnesotans 4. Can search multiple libraries and databases at once	OCLC Formerly: Fretwell-Downing Informatics	15	Active
2006	E-library for Global Welfare http://www.bath.ac.uk/gwlibrary/	International & Comparative	1. Provides a collection of online resources for international and comparative policy	Open University, University of Sheffield, University of Bath & STAKES	14	Active

3. for the sharing of knowledge, interoperability and best practice guidelines
4. Facilitates the use of well formed and useful metadata throughout our region

109

| 2006 | Intute (Closed on July, 2011, details of project can be found in UK Web Archive) http://www.intute.ac.uk/ | Multi-Subject (Engineering, Mathematics, Computing, Agriculture, Law, Physical Science, Social Science, Management, Biological Science, Geography, Medicine) | 1. It is a free online service 2. Provides access to the best Web resources for education and research 3. Subject specialists select and evaluate the websites in our database and write high quality descriptions of the resources 4. Allows access to both subject-specific and cross-subject resources | Policy Analysis, Research & Teaching | analysis, research and teaching 2. A collaborative effort of academics from different universities | Joint Information Systems Committee (JISC) (UK Higher Education) | Finland. | 5 | Closed |
| 2006 | TechXtra http://www. | Engineering, | 1. Offers free service to find subject based different | | | Institute for Computer Based | | 9 | Closed |

	techxtra.ac.uk/		Mathematics and Computing	online information resources 2. Cross searches different collections relevant to engineering, mathematics and computing, 3. Also provides different extra services (i.e. Discovery Guides, Design Data, Newsletters, E-journal Search, Jobs, Industry News, Bookstore, Internet Tutorials, Manufacturing, Gateways, Sci-Tech Library, News Highlights, Repository cross-search, Patents & Standards search etc.	Learning (ICBL) and the Library of Heriot Watt University	
2007	Clio-Online: Historical Resources in the Internet http://www.clio-online.de/site/lang__en-US/1/Default.aspx	History	1. It is a central Internet gateway for historical scholarship in teaching and research 2. Enables efficient access to the diverse range of historical online resources available to scholars and teachers 3. Performs meta-search	Clio-online	13 Active

2007	Financial Resources on the Internet *http://people.ischool. berkeley.edu/~hal/ pages/finance.html*	Economics, Finance	1. Provides economic and financial data and services 2. Gives links to online financial information resources 3. Offers access to market information and different search engines	Individual Hal R. Varian	13	Active (Not Updated)
2007	German Education Portal *http://www.fachportal-paedagogik.de/start_e.html*	Education	1. Offers central access point to professional educational information in Germany 2. Provides scholarly information to professionals engaged in educational research and practice through many pedagogical databases 3. Offers open access to scientific resources 4. Created German Education Index (a reference system) and a subject directory 5. Provides meta-search facility across a large number of pedagogical databases	German Institute for International Educational Research (DIPF)	13	Active

| 2007 | Internet Crossroads in Social Science Data http://www.disc.wisc.edu/newcrossroads/index.asp | Social Science | 1. Provides online resources related to social science research data locally and globally 2. Contains over 1000 annotated links 3. Provides updates about research data | Data & Information Service Centre (DISC) and University of Wisconsin-Madison | 13 | Active |
| 2007 | Science Accelerator http://www.scienceaccelerator.gov/ | Science (R&D results, project descriptions, accomplishments) | 1. Empowers users to search, via a single query in science, including R&D results, project descriptions, accomplishments, and more 2. It was developed to made available as a free public service 3. Facilitates searching multiple information resources in parallel 4. Provides superior access to the highest quality scientific and technical information | U.S. Department of Energy, Office of Scientific and Technical Information (OSTI) | 8 | Closed |

2007	WorldWideScience. org: The global science gateway http://worldwide science.org/	Science Subjects (Global science gateway comprised of national and international scientific databases and portals)	1. Comprises of national and international scientific databases and portals 2. Accelerates scientific discovery and progress by providing one-stop searching of databases around the world 3. Provides real-time searching and translation of globally-dispersed multilingual scientific literature	Office of the Scientific and Technical Information, US Dept. of Energy & the British Library	13 Active
2008	OFFSTATS: Official Statistics on Web http://www.offstats. auckland.ac.nz/	Statistics	1. Provides access to free statistics from official sources on the web 2. Web links are arranged by country, region or subject 3. Can be searched by a single category, or a combination of categories	University of Auckland Library	9 Closed
2008	Visual Arts Data Service (VADS) http://www.vads. ac.uk/index.php	Visual Arts	1. Provides online resource for visual arts 2. Builds up a portfolio of visual art collections	University for the Creative Arts, Farnham Campus	12 Active

Development of Subject Gateways Across the Ages 115

| 2009 | Archaeology Data Service (ADS) http://archaeologydataservice.ac.uk/ | Archaeology | 1. It supports research, learning and teaching with freely available, high quality and dependable digital resources
2. Promotes good practice in the use of digital data in archaeology
3. Provides technical advice to the research community and supports the deployment of digital technologies
3. Offers advice and guidance to the visual arts research, teaching and learning comprising over 100,000 free images and copyright cleared for use in academics in UK. | The University of York, Departments of Archaeology | 11 | Active |
| 2009 | Civil Rights Litigation Clearinghouse http://www.clearinghouse.net/ | Civil Rights | 1. Collects and analyses documents and information from civil rights cases across the United States
2. Dedicated to cases seeking policy or operational change | University of Michigan Law School | 11 | Active |

| 2009 | Communication and Media Studies (Renamed Intute which was closed on July, 2011, details of project can be found in UK Web Archive) http://www.intute.ac.uk/communication/ | Mass Communication studies | 1. Provides information on communication and media studies
2. Subject specialist on the subject finds and reviews the best web resources available on internet for studies and research
3. Can be searched through keywords or can be search by subject category
4. Assembled a number of special case collections
5. Records are organized by case category
3. Information accessible to scholars, teachers, students, policymakers, advocates, and the public at large | Joint Information Systems Committee (JISC) (UK Higher Education) | 2 | Closed |
| 2009 | Law and Legal http://www.lawandlegal.co.uk | Law | 1. Provides useful information on many issues related to UK law
2. Provides guidance to the legal career aspirants
3. Provides legal services to different regions of UK | Law and Legal, UK | 11 | Active |

Development of Subject Gateways Across the Ages 117

| 2009 | Political Science Resources http://www.politics resources.net/ | Political Science | 1. Provides information resources on Politics and Government mainly election data of UK and USA
2. Customized links are attached with the different subject category related to political science | Richard Kimber | 11 | Active |
| 2009 | Psychology (Renamed Intute which was closed on July, 2011, details of project can be found in UK Web Archive) http://www.intute.ac.uk/psychology/ | Psychology | 1. Provides free access to high quality Psychology resources on the Internet
2. Resources have been evaluated and categorized by subject specialists based at UK universities
3. Gateway can be searched through by putting keywords search engine or can directly browse the category related to psychology | Joint Information Systems Committee (JISC) (UK Higher Education) | 2 | Closed |
| 2010 | Diagnostic Enhancement of Confidence by an International Distributed Environment (DECIDE) http://www.eu-decide.eu | Medical Science | 1. Implemented an integrated e-Infrastructure and user-friendly, ubiquitous services early diagnosis of Alzheimer's and other | Consortium GARR | 10 | Active |

			neurodegenerative diseases 2. Some DECIDE publications are available in open access on the ZENODO website 3. It also offers the opportunity to host on such repository all open access publications on the said subject	
2010	Open Journal Access System (OJAS) http://www.inflibnet.ac.in/ojs/	Multi-Subject	1. Provides information about INFLIBNET Centre, Ahmedabad 2. Uses 'Open Journal Systems' software developed, supported, and freely distributed under the GNU General Public License	8 Closed#
2011	IREON: The International Relations and Area Studies Gateway https://www.ireon-portal.eu/	Political Science	1. Offers bibliographic references, full-text documents and treaties on International Relations and Area Studies IREON 2. It is a network of libraries and documentation departments of 12 research	9 Active

| 2011 | Online Reference Zone: A Gateway to Reference Resources in Science & Technology http://www.isibang.ac.in/~library/onlinerz/index2.html | Science and Technology | 1. Provides online open access reference resources in science and technology
2. Gateway is divided into different subject category (i.e. Physics, Chemistry, Mathematics, Statistics, Engineering and Technology) with which reference links are added to get actual information
3. Federated search facility is also provided
3. Provides five bibliographic databases and nine language European Thesaurus on International Relations and Area Studies for helping the user organizations | Indian Statistical Institute, Bangalore | 9 | Active# |
|---|---|---|---|---|---|---|
| 2011 | Rice Knowledge Management Portal (RKMP) http://www.rkmp.co.in/ | Agriculture (Rice) | 1. Provides comprehensive and qualitative information on Rice
2. This knowledge portal can be accessed on smart phones and tablets | Indian Institute of Rice Research, Indian Council of Agricultural Research (ICAR) | 9 | Active# |

| 2012 | Board of Governors of the Federal Reserve System http://www.federalreserve.gov/econresdata/statisticsdata.htm | Economics and Banking | 1. Provides a detailed look at the structure, responsibilities, and operations of the Federal Reserve System
2. Reflects changes in monetary, regulatory, and other policy areas. Incorporates major changes in the law and in the structure of the financial system
3. Also provides statistical digest and data on economic research | Federal Reserve Board | 8 | Active |
| 2012 | Consortium for Educational Communication (CEC) http://cec.nic.in/Pages/Home.aspx | Educational Communication Social Sciences | 1. Addressing the needs of Higher Education through Television and Information Communication Technology (ICT)
2. Disseminates educational | University Grants Commission, Ministry of HRD, Govt. of India | 8 | Active# |

| 2012 | Indian Library Association-LIS Gateway http://www.ilaindia.net | Library and Information Science | 1. Provides information on all aspects of library and information science
2. Links are arranged alphabetically under the broad subject category | Indian Library Association | 8 | Active # |
| 2012 | INFOPORT: INFLIBNET Subject Gateway for Indian Electronic-Resources http://infoport.inflibnet.ac.in | Multi-Subject | 1. Promotes open access to Indian scholarly content
2. Designed and developed to serve as a gateway to Indian scholarly content
3. Supports search, browse and multiple listing
4. Selectively catalogues online resources of Indian origin | INFLIBNET Centre, Ahmedabad | 8 | Active # |

(continued from previous row) knowledge through the mode of Television
3. Produces educational programmes (Audio/Visual and Web Based)
4. Provides e-education, Vyas Higher Education Channel and e-Knowledge Resources

| 2012 | Lawlinks http://www.kent.ac.uk/library/subjects/lawlinks/ | Law | 1. Helps students to find links of different websites to get access to online legal resources
2. Users have the flexibility to use the search box to search the whole group of sites | University of Kent | 8 | Active |
| 2013 | Subject Information Gateway in Information Technology (SIGIT) http://www.itsubjectgateway.info | Information Technology (IT) | 1. First full-fledged subject information gateway exclusively in the field of Information Technology (IT)
2. Provides systematic resource discovery
3. Can be searched by keywords or browse by subject area
4. Covers almost all areas of information technology
5. Cater the information needs | SIGIT | 7 | Active# |

5. Selects contents through elaborate process of evaluation and testing
6. It does not cover resources other than those originated in India

| 2013 | Discover Society: Measured – Factual – Critical http://discoversociety.org | Social Work | 1. Provides articles, commentary, viewpoint, policy briefing on social research and policy analysis 2. Includes author index and topic index 3. Articles are covered by a Creative Commons license 6. Contents of the resources are regularly updated 7. Incorporates new and innovative features of the IT professionals and members of academic community | Madidus | 7 | Active |
| 2013 | e-PgPathshala: A Gateway to all Post Graduate Courses http://epgp.inflibnet.ac.in/ | Multi-Subject | 1. Develops and provides e-contents on 71 subjects at postgraduate level 2. High quality, curriculum-based, interactive content in different subjects across all disciplines are being developed 3. Contents are arranged as per subject category | INFLIBNET | 7 | #Active |

| 2013 | Karger Open Access : Searchable Gateway http://www.karger.com/OpenAccess | Bio-medical Articles | 1. Provides collection of open access online searchable articles
2. Contains information about Journals, Books, Collection and Subject Guide | S. Karger AG | 7 | Active |
| 2013 | UK Data Service https://www.ukdataservice.ac.uk/ | Social and Economic Data Resources | 1. Explores the UK's largest collection of social, economic and population data resources
2. Collection includes major UK government-sponsored surveys, cross-national surveys, longitudinal studies, UK census data, international aggregate, business data, and qualitative data etc.
3. Provides access to high-quality local, regional, national and international social and economic data
4. Supports for policy-relevant research in the higher education, public and commercial sectors | University of Essex, University of Manchester and Jisc | 7 | Active |

2014	All India Libraries and Librarians Management Information System (AILLMIS) http://www.aillmis.net/index.php	Library and Information Science	1. Aims to interlinks and integrate all the libraries and library professionals from all over India 2. Developed an interface of Indian Knowledge Grid Network (INKOGNET) of Libraries and Librarians 5. Offers guidance and training for the development of skills in data use	PD &UGC	4	Closed#
2014	LIS Learning http://lislearning.in/	Library and Information Science	1. Uploads material created by Lislearning and for library professionals in English Language 2. Helps to impart LIS education in all types of library professionals 3. The site has been divided in to various categories such as Faculty Corner, Professionals Corner, Researchers Corner, Students Corner etc. to meet the different information requirements of LIS community		6	Active#

| 2015 | Finding Statistics and Data http://guides.lib.umich.edu/c.php?g=283068 | Statistics | 1. Helps in finding statistics produced by government on a wide variety of topics
2. Provide link to 'Statista' - a portal for current statistics from private and government sources on wide range of topics including technology, health, public opinion, and market research
3. Provides access to Data-Planet Statistical Datasets and ProQuest Statistical Insight | University of Michigan, School of Information and Library Studies | 5 | Active |

Note: # Indian Subject Gateway

REFERENCES

1. Middleton, M., Edwards, S. L., & Collins, J. (1999, November). Development of an Internet site evaluation tool for use by information management students. In *Mid-Year Conference for American Society for Information Science* (May 24-26). Pasadena, California. Retrieved from *https://eprints.qut.edu.au/107/1/ASIS_99MY.pdf*

2. Kanetkar, J. (2014). Development of subject gateways: A status update. *DESIDOC Journal of Library & Information Technology, 34*(5), 367-375. doi: 10.14429/djlit.34.5807

7
Problems Faced by Subject Gateways

Since the inception, subject gateways across the world have been facing different problems. These problems (both administrative and technical issues) have come to the forefront along with its gradual development.

- Awareness or operational knowledge of searching information through internet differs from one information seeker to another. It is one of the greatest challenges before the information professionals to develop an information search and retrieval tool which could satisfy all information seekers irrespective of their knowledge level. Therefore, extensive orientation, including promotion of subject gateways **(Bawden & Robinson, 2002)**[1] is essential for making it effective and popular.

- Creation of quality contents for subject gateways requires engagement of subject experts. Moreover, selecting, deselecting, capturing, processing and disseminating of web contents are labour intensive job. Update of existing links and web contents requires engagement of trained manpower. Whatever may be case, huge amount of money is involved in running a subject gateway. Therefore sustainability is one of the major issues before any active gateway. Operational sustainability **(Freshwater, 2002; Huxley & Joyce, 2004)** [2 & 3] especially future financial sustenance **(Bradshaw, 1997; Dempsey, 2000)** [4 & 5] is the burning problem of any operational subject gateway.

- Value of a subject gateway depends on quality and coverage of its contents. In quality-controlled subject gateways considerable amount of human efforts are given for selection of quality resources. In order to ensure good collection regular checking and update is needed. But absences of trained manpower for the said job lead to the closure of many subject gateways.

- Gateways have been introducing many alternate services in order to financially sustain themselves **(Dempsey, 2000)**[6]. They were trying to reduce funding burden by way of collaboration and commercial engagement.

- Subject gateways are not able to provide commercially subscribed documents (e-journals and databases) freely to all information seekers. It has a limitation that it can only provide open source web contents to all of its users **(Fredline & Reis, 1999)**[7].

- Most of the subject gateways were developed by a small group of subject specialists and information professionals of an institution with subject relevance. Although collaboration is increasing, still few gateways are maintained by individuals **(Robinson & Bawden, 1999)**[8].

- It has been observed through my survey that there have been many subject gateways on same subject. International consensus in the development of subject gateway is needed to avoid repetition **(Campbell, 2000)**[9]. Thus it will save time, money and manpower.

- Many subject gateways are not designed in accordance with user orientation, predominant usage and needs of the community. Therefore, they have been closed after few years of existence **(Rowley, 2000)**[10].

- In order to maximise search output, interoperability among different subject gateways is the need of the hour. It is beyond doubt that the need for integrating different subject vocabularies in the networked environment is essential **(Chan & Zeng, 2002)**[11]. Now-a-days, the Dublin Core Metadata element set has been used to enhance document retrieval and navigation, and it also helps to allow interoperability **(Thirion, Loosli, Douyère, & Darmoni, 2003)**[12].

- When keyword indexing is the only option for searching in a subject gateway, then spelling variation, updated terminology, foreign language phrases and contextually ambiguous terms could lead to false positive retrieval. It is one of the regular operational difficulties that most of the subject gateways face everyday. A thesaurus of subject terms could enhance searching precision by eliminating false leads. As a user oriented classification on the Web, folksonomy emerged as another viable approach **(Uddin, Mezbah-ul-Islam, & Haque, 2006)**[13].

- In order to disseminate information to all section of the society, there have been great demands from information seekers for developing subject gateways in regional languages. It will help to reduce the knowledge gap among information seekers of the lower section of the society (i.e. General information seekers, farmers, workers etc.)

REFERENCE

1. Bawden, D., & Robinson, L. (2002). Internet subject gateways revisited. *International Journal of Information Management, 22*(2), 157-162. doi: 10.1016/S0268-4012(01)00051-2

2. Freshwater, M. (2002). *Subject Gateways: An investigation into their role in the information environment (with particular reference to AERADE, the subject gateway for aerospace and defence)*. (Master's dissertation, University of Central England, Birmingham).

3. Huxley, L., & Joyce, A. (2004). A social science gateway in a shifting digital world: Shaping SOSIG for users' needs of the future. *Online Information Review, 28*(5), 328-337. doi: 10.1108/14684520410564253

4. Bradshaw, R. (1997).Introducing ADAM: A gateway to internet resources in art, design, architecture and media. *Program, 31*(3), 251-267. doi: 10.1108/eum0000000006889

5. Dempsey, L. (2000). The subject gateway: experiences and issues based on the emergence of the Resource Discovery Network. *Online Information Review, 24*(1), 8-23. doi: 10.1108/14684520010323029

6. Dempsey, L. (2000). The subject gateway: experiences and issues based on the emergence of the Resource Discovery Network. *Online Information Review, 24*(1), 8-23. doi: 10.1108/14684520010323029

7. Fredline, S., & Reis, B. (1999). Infoquest: Collaborative development of a subject resource gateway. *New Review of Information Networking, 5*(1), 125-130. doi: 10.1080/13614579909516941

8. Robinson, L. & Bawden, D. (1999). Internet subject gateways. *International Journal of Information Management, 19*(6), 511-522. Retrieved from *https://openaccess.city.ac.uk/id/eprint/3184/1/Internet%20subject%20gateways.pdf* accessed on 21.04.2020

9. Campbell, D. (2000). Australian subject gateways: political and strategic issues. *Online Information Review, 24*(1), 73-77. doi:10.1108/14684520010320266

10. Rowley, J. (2000). Knowledge organisation for a new millennium: Principles and processes. *Journal of Knowledge Management, 4*(3), 217-223. doi:10.1108/13673270010350011

11. Chan, L. M., & Zeng, M. L. (2002). Ensuring interoperability among subject vocabularies and knowledge organization schemes: A methodological analysis. *IFLA Journal, 28*(5-6), 323-327. Retrieved from *http://files.eric.ed.gov/fulltext/ED472886.pdf* accessed on 21.04.2020

12. Thirion, B., Loosli, G., Douyère, M., & Darmoni, S. J. (2003). Metadata element set in a quality-controlled subject gateway: A step to a health semantic web. *Studies in Health Technology and Informatics*, 707-712.

13. Uddin, M. N., Mezbah-ul-Islam, M., & Haque, K. M. G. (2006). Information description and discovery method using classification structures in web. *Malaysian Journal of Library and Information Science, 11*(2), 1-20. Retrieved from *https://mjlis.um.edu.my/article/view/7828* accessed on 21.04.2020

8
How to Develop a Subject Gateway : A Step-by-Step Approach

- Step 1: Needs Assessment
- Step 2: Literature Review
- Step 3: Study of Subject
- Step 4: Creating a Taxonomy
- Step 5: Fundraising
- Step 6: Selection of Place, Hardware and Software
- Step 7: Installation of software
- Step 8: Selection of Theme and Arrangements of Blocks
- Step 9: Development of Web Pages
- Step 10: Demonstration for Feedbacks
- Step 11: Regular update: Software, Contents and Links

8.1. NEEDS ASSESSMENT

Need assessment is conducted before the actual project work begins. It is a simple process to find out the gap between current and desired conditions expected by the end user of the proposed project. It can be done through an end-user survey either through interview methods or through a pre-formatted questionnaire.

8.2. LITERATURE REVIEW

Once you are sure about the desired needs of your end-user from the proposed system, you have to consider all possible options available before you for developing such a system. If you think that developing a subject gateway is your best alternative, then you can go for a detailed literature review on your chosen subject on which you are going to develop your subject gateway. Apart from published literature, you have to consider for other existing websites, databases and computer systems on your chosen subject. Main intention of this kind of review is to access the level of exploration already done on the selected subject.

8.3. STUDY OF SUBJECT

When you are going to develop a subject gateway on a new subject which may not be your area of study, still you have to develop a comprehensive knowledge on that subject. Otherwise you may not be able to develop the same. Therefore, you need to study the new subject in a scientific manner popularly known as "Study of Subject". It will help you to have a comprehensive knowledge on the new subject.

8.4. CREATING TAXONOMY

After a comprehensive study of subject, you need to create Taxonomy of relevant Terms or Subject Heading. It will help you to get easy access to information and its retrieval from the subject gateway. The proposed subject gateway can be searched easily if the taxonomy follows hierarchical-enumerative structure. Therefore, creating a well organised taxonomy is of prime importance for constructing a subject gateway. You may create individual web pages with each of the Subject Terms or Subject Headings which are commonly known as Tags.

8.5. FUNDRAISING

You can to go ahead with your project further unless you raise fund for your project. You have to convince the funding agency about the prospect of your project. Your previous work on Need Assessment and Literature Review on your project may be helpful in justifying your claim before the funding agency. Your funding agency may be your Institution, Government Departments or may be Private Organization. Don't get disappointed, if you are unable to raise funds for your project despite your best efforts. Now you have to do re-planning of your project and develop a prototype model of your subject gateway with your own fund and place the same before the funding agencies for their funding approval.

8.6. SELECTION OF PLACE, HARDWARE AND SOFTWARE

Now you have to select the place of your project and also the hardware and software for the proposed subject gateway. Your choices will largely depend on the funds available for your project. If you have limited or no funds for your project, you may develop the prototype in your home computer or laptop with open source software available in the market.

8.7. INSTALLATION OF SOFTWARE

If you are not a computer professional or a layman not confident about the software, still you can develop a subject gateway with open source software with little or no training with the following software. You need an open source solution stack/ software stack for constructing a local web server on which you have to develop a web portal with an open source Content Management System (CMS).

I have used XAMPP software stack, which is a free and open-source web server solution stack package, can be used in different platform (i.e. Windows, Linux, Mac OS etc.). It was developed by Apache Friends. XAMPP follows WAMP /

LAMP stack which helps a developer to install the stack easily on his/her operating system. XAMPP consisting of:

X - Stands for Cross Platform (Windows, Linux, Mac OS etc.)
A - Stands for Apache HTTP Server
M - Stands for MariaDB (formerly MySQL) Database
P - Stands for PHP Programming Language
P - Stands for PERL Programming Language

For installing XAMPP to your computer, you need to go to the website of Apache Friends (*https://www.apachefriends.org/index.html*) and select the suitable Operating System for which you want to download the XAMPP stack software. It requires one zip, tar, 7z, or .exe file to be downloaded and run. In addition, Microsoft Visual C++ 2017 Redistributable need to be pre-installed in your system for Windows version of XAMPP.

In addition, you can download any add-on CMS like Drupal, Zoomla or WordPress from Bitnami (*https://bitnami.com/stack/xampp#drupal*) and installed it on XAMPP. As most of the actual web server operation follows the same software module that of XAMPP, changeover from local Test Server to actual Production Server becomes very easy.

8.8. SELECTION OF THEME AND ARRANGEMENTS OF BLOCKS

Depending on the CMS, you have to choose a particular theme for the whole website because all web-pages will be arranged as per the chosen theme. For example, there are different theme available linked to a particular version of Drupal. You have to choose and enable a particular theme among several illustrated themes available, for your proposed web-site. Moreover, an administrative theme needs to be enabled for editing or creating content.

As per the enabled theme, you have to select different blocks (i.e. Header, Help, Content, Sidebars, and Footers etc.)

as per the requirements and configure them at suitable places of the web pages.

8.9. DEVELOPMENT OF WEB PAGES

Before you could develop an actual web page and place the same under a particular menu, you need to know the type of Content Types (i.e. Article, Basic Page and Forum Topic) that you can create in Drupal. After creating a particular web-page, it needs to be placed under proper type of Menu (i.e. Main Menu, Management Menu, Navigation Menu and User Menu.)

A typical Article page under Main menu consists of a Title, Body (Write up, Tables References, Links etc.), Tags, Image, Language, Parent Item/ Node (under which the page to be created) and Weight (for determining the place of the particular web-page under a particular parent node. One can also include metadata element with a particular web-pages. The web-page need to be saved and published otherwise it can not be seen. Apart from core modules in Drupal, there are different Contributed Modules available in Drupal Site (*https://www.drupal.org/project/project_module*) which can be downloaded and installed in your CMS as per your requirements. When you are ready with your development, you can test it with localhost by typing (*http://127.0.0.1/drupal/*) in the address bar of your web browser.

8.10. DEMONSTRATION FOR FEEDBACKS

You can demonstrate your website to your end user either through localhost (127.0.0.1) or it can be mounted on live production server for their feedback. You can use printed or web based questionnaire for their feedback. As per their feedback, you can always update or modify your site as per the requirements. Those subject gateways which are regularly updated and provide qualitative contents to the end user are considered to be good and last long.

8.11. REGULAR UPDATE : SOFTWARE, CONTENTS AND LINKS

Thereafter the software used in your subject gateway need to be regularly updated as soon as any software update or security update is available. Apart from this you need to periodically back up your system to counter any unwanted system crash or faults. Periodic backup and restore of your database and files will help you to migrating data from or to another website developed with Drupal CMS. Contents of your web pages also require regular update by subject experts. Subject gateways provide various types of web links to supplement the content of the web pages. Therefore, periodic link checking is absolute necessity for keeping the subject gateway relevant to the user.

Bibliography

Anil Hirwade, M. (2011). A study of metadata standards. *Library Hi Tech News, 28*(7), 18-25. doi: 10.1108/07419051111184052

Banik, M. (2001). *Information services for jute research institutes in Bangladesh: a critical study of the present scenario and a plan for future development* (Doctoral dissertation, Jadavpur University).

Bawden, D., & Robinson, L. (2002). Internet subject gateways revisited. *International Journal of Information Management, 22*(2), 157-162. doi: 10.1016/S0268-4012(01)00051-2

Bhardwaj, R. K. (2013). Leveraging access to e-resources through gateway: A case study at St. Stephen's College, Delhi. *DESIDOC Journal of Library & Information Technology, 33*(5), 418-425. Retrieved from https://www.researchgate.net/profile/Raj_Bhardwaj/publication/270492284_Leveraging_Access_to_E-resources_through_Gateway_A_Case_Study_at_St_Stephen's_College_Delhi/links/55ea98fa08ae21d099c45840.pdf accessed on 06.05.2020

Bradshaw, R. (1997).Introducing ADAM: A gateway to internet resources in art, design, architecture and media. *Program, 31*(3), 251-267. doi: 10.1108/eum0000000006889

Campbell, D. (2000). Australian subject gateways: political and strategic issues. *Online Information Review, 24*(1), 73-77. doi: 10.1108/14684520010320266

Caswell, J. V. (2006). Leveraging resources in a library gateway. *Library Hi Tech, 24*(1), 142-152. doi: 10.1108/07378830510636391

Caswell, J. V., & Wynstra, J. D. (2010). Improving the search experience: Federated search and the library gateway. *Library Hi Tech, 28*(3), 391-401. doi: 10.1108/07378831011076648

Chan, L. M., & Zeng, M. L. (2002). Ensuring interoperability among subject vocabularies and knowledge organization schemes: A methodological analysis. *IFLA Journal, 28*(5-6), 323-327. Retrieved from *http://files.eric.ed.gov/fulltext/ED472886.pdf* accessed on 03.05.2020

Clark, N., & Frost, D. (2002). User-centred evaluation and design: A subject gateway perspective. In *11th VALA Conference, Melbourne* (pp. 6-8). Retrieved from *http://www.vala.org.au/vala2002/2002pdf/38ClaFro.pdf* accessed on 03.05.2020

Day, M., Koch, T., & Neuroth, H. (2005). Searching and browsing multiple subject gateways in the Renardus service. Retrieved from *http://opus.bath.ac.uk/14366/1/day-renardus-paper-v2.pdf* accessed on 03.05.2020

Dempsey, L. (2000). The subject gateway: experiences and issues based on the emergence of the Resource Discovery Network. *Online Information Review, 24*(1), 8-23. doi: 10.1108/14684520010323029

Dixon, T., Melve, I., Meneses, R., & Verschuren, T. (1998). Building large-scale information services: Tools and experiences from the DESIRE project. *Computer Networks and ISDN Systems, 30*(16), 1559-1569. doi: 10.1016/S0169-7552(98)00190-1

Fredline, S., & Reis, B. (1999). Infoquest: Collaborative development of a subject resource gateway. *New Review of Information Networking, 5*(1), 125-130. doi: 10.1080/13614579909516941

Freshwater, M. (2002). *Subject gateways: An investigation into their role in the information environment (with particular reference to AERADE, the subject gateway for aerospace and defence.* (Masters Dissertation, University of Central England, Birmingham). Retrieved from *http://citeseerx.ist.psu.edu/viewdoc/download?doi=10.1.1.202.5134&rep=rep1&type=pdf* accessed on 07.04.2020

Gul, S. (2009). *Development of web resources in select fields of social sciences with a view to design a model subject gateway* (Doctoral dissertation, University of Kashmir).

Heery, R. (2000). Information gateways: Collaboration on content. *Online Information Review, 24*(1), 40-45. doi: 10.1108/14684520010320077

Heron, S. J., & Hanson, A. (2003). From subject gateways to portals: The role of metadata in accessing international research. Retrieved from *http://scholarcommons.usf.edu/cgi/viewcontent.cgi?article=1011&context=dean_cbcs* accessed on 03.05.2020

Hickey, T. B. (2000). CORC: A system for gateway creation. *Online Information Review, 24*(1), 49-56. doi: 10.1108/14684520010371549

Higher Education Funding Council for England. (1993). *Joint Funding Council's Libraries Review Group: Report (The Follett Report).* Retrieved from *http://www.ukoln.ac.uk/services/papers/follett/report/* accessed on 19.04.2020

Huang, R., & Liu, C. (2007). An investigation and analysis of e-services in major subject based information gateways in the world. In Integration and innovation orient to e-society Volume 2 (pp. 209-217). Springer Boston, MA. doi: 10.1007/978-0-387-75494-9_26

Huxley, L. (2001). Renardus: Fostering collaboration between academic subject gateways in Europe. *Online Information Review, 25*(2), 121-127. doi: 10.1108/14684520110390060.

Huxley, L., & Joyce, A. (2004). A social science gateway in a shifting digital world: Shaping SOSIG for users' needs of the future. *Online Information Review, 28*(5), 328-337. doi: 10.1108/14684520410564253

Jefcoate, G. (2006). Gabriel: Gateway to Europe's national libraries. *Program, 40*(4), 325-333. doi: 10.1108/00330330610707908.

Kaczmarek, J., & ChiatNaun, C. (2005). A state-wide meta-search service using OAI-PMH and Z39.50. *Library Hi Tech, 23*(4), 576-586. doi: 10.1108/07378830510636355

Kanetkar, J. (2014). Development of subject gateways: A status update. *DESIDOC Journal of Library & Information Technology, 34*(5). 367-375. doi: 10.14429/djlit.34.5807

Koch, T. (2000). Quality-controlled subject gateways: definitions, typologies, empirical overview. *Online Information Review, 24*(1), 24-34. doi: 10.1108/14684520010320040

Krishnamurthy, M. (2005, July). Designing a gateway interface: Conceptual framework for library and information science. *Information Studies, 11*(3), 195-204.

Kuk, G. (1999). Social science information gateway for psychology: A utility test of SOSIG. Social Science Computer Review, 17(4), 451-454. doi: 10.1177/089443939901700405

Kumar, S., & Singh, M. (2011). Access and use of electronic information resources by scientists of national physical laboratory in India: A case study. *Singapore Journal of Library and Information Management*, 40, 33-49. Retrieved from *https://www.researchgate.net/profile/Shailendra_ Kumar12/publication/230881125_Access_and_use_of_electronic_ information_resources_by_scientists_of_National_Physical_Laboratory_ in_India_A_case_study/links/0fcfd505ae3f8b352b000000.pdf* accessed on 06.05.2020

Lalhmachhuana. (2006, November). Subject information gateways as the scholars' pathways for avoiding the internet chaos: New prospects and challenges for LIS professionals. In Manoj Kumar K. (Eds.), *4th*

Convention planner-2006: Digital preservation, management, and access to information in the twenty first century, Mizoram University, Aizawl (pp.418-429). Ahmedabad: INFLIBNET Centre. Retrieved from http://ir.inflibnet.ac.in:8080/ir/ViewerJS/#../bitstream/1944/1324/1/418-429.pdf accessed on 04.05.2020

Mackie, M., & Burton, P. F. (1999). The use and effectiveness of the eLib subject gateways: A preliminary investigation. *Program, 33*(4), 327-337. doi: 10.1108/eum0000000006922

Macleod, R., Kerr, L., & Guyon, A. (1998). The EEVL approach to providing a subject based information gateway for engineers. *Program, 32*(3), 205-223. doi: 10.1108/eum0000000006901

Madhusudhan, M. (2007).Internet use by research scholars in University of Delhi, India., *Library Hi Tech News*, 24(8), 36-42.doi:10.1108/07419050710836036

Mahemei, L. K., Thulasi, K., & Rajashekar, T.B. (2005). Approaches to taxonomy development: Some experiences in the context of an academic institute information portal. In: *International conference on information management in a knowledge society*, 21-25 February, 2005, Mumbai, India,(pp. 315-326.) Retrieved from http://eprints.iisc.ac.in/2853/1/icim-paper1.pdf accessed on 04.05.2020

Manivel, D. (2014). *Design and development of physics gateway: with special reference to Bharathidasan university* (Master's dissertation, Bharathidasan University). Retrieved from http://14.139.186.108/jspui/bitstream/123456789/14829/2/manivel%20final%20project1.pdf accessed on 05.05.2020

MasoomRaza, M., & Eqbal, M. (2005). Design and development of library and information science gateway: An Indian initiative. *International Information & Library Review, 37*(4), 365-374. doi: 10.1080/10572317.2005.10762694

Matthews, B., Jones, C., Puzoñ, B., Moon, J., Tudhope, D., Golub, K., & Lykke Nielsen, M. (2010, July). An evaluation of enhancing social tagging with a knowledge organization system. In V. Broughton (Ed.), *Aslib Proceedings*, (Vol. 62, No. 4/5, pp. 447-465). Emerald Group Publishing Limited. doi: 10.1108/00012531011074690

Meera, B. M., & Ummer, R. (2012). Online reference zone: A gateway to reference resources in science and technology. *SRELS Journal of Information Management, 49*(1), 55-62.doi: 10.17821/srels/2012/v49i1/43816

Middleton, M., Edwards, S. L., & Collins, J. (1999, November). Development of an Internet site evaluation tool for use by information management students. In *Mid-Year Conference for American Society for Information*

Science (May 24-26). Pasadena, California. Retrieved from *https://eprints.qut.edu.au/107/1/ASIS_99MY.pdf*

Miller, M. A., Pfeiffer, W., & Schwartz, T. (2012). The CIPRES science gateway: enabling high-impact science for phylogenetics researchers with limited resources. In *Proceedings of the 1st conference of the extreme science and engineering discovery environment: Bridging from the extreme to the campus and beyond* (p.39). ACM. doi: 10.1145/2335755.2335836

Monopoli, M., & Nicholas, D. (2001). A user evaluation of subject based information gateways: Case study ADAM. In *Aslib Proceedings* (Vol. 53, No.1, pp.39-52). MCB UP Ltd. doi: 10.1108/eum0000000007036

Morville, P. S., & Wickhorst, S. J. (1996). Building subject-specific guides to internet resources. *Internet Research, 6*(4), 27-32. doi: 10.1108/10662249610152276

Mukhopadhyay, C. (1996). *Documentation in jute technology: Its origin and development* (Doctoral dissertation, University of Calcutta).

Munshi, U. M. (2009). Building subject gateway in a shifting digital world. *DESIDOC Journal of Library & Information Technology, 29*(2), 7-14.

Neelakandan, B., Malatesh, N., Surulinathi, M., & Srinivasa, R. (2010). Designing and hosting of biotechnology gateway. *International Journal of Environmental Sciences, 1*(2), 163-175. Retrieved from *http://14.139.186.108/jspui/bitstream/123456789/4977/1/EIJES1016.pdf* accessed on 04.05.2020

Neuroth, H., & Koch, T. (2001, October). Metadata mapping and application profiles: approaches to providing the cross-searching of heterogeneous resources in the EU project Renardus. In *International Conference on Dublin Core and Metadata Applications* (pp. 122-129). National Institute of Informatics, Tokyo, Japan. Retrieved from *http://dcpapers.dublincore.org/index.php/pubs/article/viewFile/650/646* accessed on 03.05.2020

Nierstrasz, O. (1996). *W3 catalog history*. Retrieved from *http://scg.unibe.ch/archive/software/w3catalog/W3CatalogHistory.html* accessed on 19.04.2020

Niyogi, B. (1993). *Information needs in jute and allied fibre industries in India* (Doctoral dissertation, Jadavpur University).

Peereboom, M. (2000). DutchESS: Dutch electronic subject service – a Dutch national collaborative effort. *Online Information Review, 24*(1), 46-49. doi:10.1108/14684520010320095

Place, E. (2000). International collaboration on internet subject gateways. *IFLA Journal, 26*(1), 52-56. doi: 10.1177/034003520002600108

Pommi, S. (2011). *Developing a gateway for world digital libraries: A study*

(Masters dissertation, Bharathidasan University).

Powell, A. (2001). An OAI approach to sharing subject gateway content. In *Tenth International World Wide Web Conference (WWW10)*. University of Bath. Retrieved from *https://researchportal.bath.ac.uk/files/617071/Powell.pdf* accessed on 03.05.2020

Price, A. (2000). NOVAGate: A nordic gateway to electronic resources in the forestry, veterinary and agricultural sciences. *Online Information Review*, 24(1), 69-73. doi: 10.1108/14684520010320158

Priestley, A. (1998). Vantage points: Information gateways for business in the Yorkshire and Humber Region. *New Review of Information Networking*, 4(1), 213-216. doi: 10.1080/13614579809516930

Rajashekara, G. R. (2010). BT-gate: A subject gateway of biotechnology. *SRELS Journal of Information Management*, 47(4), 427-436. doi: 10.17821/srels/2010/v47i4/44967

Robinson, L. & Bawden, D. (1999). Internet subject gateways. *International Journal of Information Management*, 19(6), 511-522. Retrieved from *http://openaccess.city.ac.uk/3184/1/Internet%20subject%20gateways.pdf* accessed on 06.05.2020

Rowley, J. (2000). Knowledge organisation for a new millennium: Principles and processes. *Journal of Knowledge Management*, 4(3), 217-223. doi: 10.1108/13673270010350011

Sadeh, T. (2004). The challenge of meta-searching. *New Library World*, 105(3/4), 104-112. doi: 10.1108/03074800410526721

Sanyal, S. (2019). *Design and development of 'Jute-Gate': A prototype model of subject gateway on Jute information* (Doctoral dissertation, University of Calcutta).

Singh, A., & Gautam, J. N. (2003). Himalayan information subject gateway in digital era: A proposal for its development. *DESIDOC Journal of Library & Information Technology*, 23(2), 3-9. doi: 10.14429/dbit.23.2.3593

Sladen, C. & Spence, M. (2000). Hand picked for quality – a reflection on biz/ed. *Library Consortium Management*, 2(2), 35-43.

Sreenivasulu, V. (2000). The role of a digital librarian in the management of digital information systems. *The Electronic Llibrary*, 18(1), 12-20. Retrieved from *http://eprints.rclis.org/6502/1/role-DL-DIS.pdf* accessed on 07.05.2020

Sureshkumar, S. (2012). *Design and development of a physics subject gateway at Bharathidasan university library* (Masters dissertation, Bharathidasan University).

Thirion, B., Loosli, G., Douyère, M., & Darmoni, S. J. (2003). Metadata element set in a quality-controlled subject gateway: A step to a health semantic web. *Studies in Health Technology and Informatics,* 707-712. Retrieved from *https://www.researchgate.net/profile/Gaelle_Loosli/publication/8969250_Metadata_element_set_in_a_Quality-Controlled_Subject_Gateway_a_step_to_an_health_semantic_Web/links/0deec533e7a26350c6000000.pdf* accessed on 03.05.2020

Thirupathi, J. (2014). *Designing the subject gateway for mathematics and statistics using Webnode* (Doctoral dissertation, Bharathidasan University). Retrieved from *http://14.139.186.108/jspui/bitstream/123456789/14831/2/thirupathi.pdf* accessed on 05.05.2020

Tiefel, V. (1991). The gateway to information: A system redefines how libraries are used. *American Libraries, 22*(9), 858-860. Retrieved from *http://www.jstor.org/stable/25632371* accessed on 26.01.2017

Tramullas, J., & Garrido, P. (2006). Constructing web subject gateways using dublin core, the resource description framework and topic maps. *Information Research, 11*(2), 1-10. Retrieved from *http://eprints.rclis.org/7540/2/paper248.pdf* accessed on 04.05.2020

Uddin, M. N., Mezbah-ul-Islam, M., & Haque, K. M. G. (2006). Information description and discovery method using classification structures in web. *Malaysian Journal of Library and Information Science, 11*(2), 1-20. Retrieved from *https://mjlis.um.edu.my/article/view/7828/5383* accessed on 04.05.2020

Vijayakumar, M., & Ganesan, A. (2006). Collaborative and interoperable subject gateways. *Information Studies, 12*(4), 213-218.

Vijayaselvi, P., & Natarajan, N. O. (2014). A study on the design, development and hosting portal subject gateway of mathematics. *Journal of Advances in Library and Information Science, 3*(3), 275-277. Retrieved from *http://www.jalis.in/pdf/pdf3-3/Vijaya.pdf* accessed on 05.05.2020

Wang, L. (2011). A study of key techniques of subject information gateway service. In *Advanced research on computer science and information engineering,* 183-187. Springer Berlin Heidelberg. doi: 10.1007/978-3-642-21411-0_30

Ward, D. (2001). Internet resource cataloging: the SUNY Buffalo Libraries' response. *OCLC Systems & Services, 17*(1), 19-26.

Wikipedia. (2020). *Charles Bachman.* Retrieved from *https://en.wikipedia.org/wiki/Charles_Bachman* on 09/04/2020

Wikipedia. (2020). *Database.* Retrieved from *https://en.wikipedia.org/wiki/Database* on 10/04/2020

Williams, M. E. (1986). Transparent information systems through gateways, front ends, intermediaries and interfaces. *Journal of the American*

Society for Information Science, 37(4), 204-214.

Williams, M. E., & Rouse, S. K. (Eds.). (1976). *Computer-readable bibliographic databases: A directory and data sourcebook*. Washington, D.C.: American Society for Information Science.

World Wide Web Foundation. (2018). *History of the web*. Retrieved from http://webfoundation.org/about/vision/history-of-the-web/ accessed on 19.04.2020

Worsfold, E. (1998). Subject gateways: Fulfilling the DESIRE for knowledge. *Computer Networks and ISDN Systems*, 30(16-18), 1479-1489. doi: 10.1016/S0169-7552(98)00185-8

Yuvaraja, R. (2014). *Design and development of subject gateway with special reference to chemistry* (Masters Dissertation, Bharathidasan University). Retrieved from http://14.139.186.108/jspui/bitstream/123456789/14830/2/R.Yuvaraja%20%202.pdf accessed on 05.05.2020

Zygogiannis, K., Papatheodorou, C., Chandrinos, K., & Makropoulos, K. (2009). Automatic web resource discovery for subject gateways. Retrieved from https://www.researchgate.net/profile/Christos_Papatheodorou/publication/255582837_Automatic_Web_Resource_Discovery_for_Subject_Gateways/links/0f31753bfcd7fa7540000000.pdf accessed on 04.05.2020